A Pair of Miracles

A Story of Autism, Faith, and Determined Parenting

Karla Akins

D0003707

Kregel
Publications

A Pair of Miracles: A Story of Autism, Faith, and Determined Parenting
© 2017 by Karla Akins

Published by Kregel Publications, a division of Kregel, Inc., 2450 Oak Industrial Dr. NE, Grand Rapids, MI 49505.

All rights reserved. No part of this book may be reproduced, stored in a retrieval system, or transmitted in any form or by any means—electronic, mechanical, photocopy, recording, or otherwise—without written permission of the publisher, except for brief quotations in reviews.

Distribution of digital editions of this book in any format via the Internet or any other means without the publisher's written permission or by license agreement is a violation of copyright law and is subject to substantial fines and penalties. Thank you for supporting the author's rights by purchasing only authorized editions.

The author and publisher are not engaged in rendering medical or psychological services, and this book is not intended as a guide to diagnose or treat medical or psychological problems. If medical, psychological, or other expert assistance is required, the reader should seek the services of a healthcare provider or certified counselor.

All Scripture quotations, unless otherwise indicated, are from the Holy Bible, New International Version®, NIV®. Copyright © 1973, 1978, 1984, 2011 by Biblica, Inc.™ Used by permission of Zondervan. All rights reserved worldwide. www.zondervan.com

Scripture quotations marked KJV are from the King James Version.

Scripture quotations marked NKJV are from the New King James Version®. Copyright © 1982 by Thomas Nelson. Used by permission. All rights reserved.

ISBN 978-0-8254-4484-5

Printed in the United States of America
17 18 19 20 21 22 23 24 25 26 / 5 4 3 2 1

To Isaiah Michael and Isaac Matthew.
I'm amazed and grateful God gave me the miracle of you.
Oh, how I love being your Motherbird.

Contents

Acknowledgments

First and foremost, this book wouldn't exist without the lives of the remarkable identical twin boys who inspired it. Isaiah and Isaac, you inspire more important lessons in me each day than I could ever begin to teach you. Thanks for giving me the time and permission to write this book. If everyone could live life with your unbridled joy and servanthood, the world would be a beautiful place.

Eddie, my dearest, most darling husband, I want the world to know how much I admire your love for our sons. Thank you for giving me time and space to write and dream. I can never express how grateful I am that you're a good daddy and an awesome grandpa.

To my sons' helpers and influences over the years: their Sunday school and church teachers, Miss Dianna, Miss Mary, Miss Judy, and other members of Christian Fellowship Church; their former caregiver, Miss Ruth; Talbot's mom, Ginger; Rhonda Bright, their special education teacher at Manchester High School; and all the staff, therapists, and teachers they've had over the years—thank you.

There are so many more people who have poured into my sons that I couldn't possibly list you all without forgetting someone. Thank you, all of you, for teaching my boys and helping them become who they are today. Please know how grateful I am for you. I know a reward is waiting for you in heaven.

Thank you to my agent, Linda Glaz of Hartline Literary Agency, for your constant encouragement and help, and my editors, Joel Armstrong, Ken Walker, and Steve Barclift, for your excellent guidance and for recognizing the potential of this book.

I owe a ton of chocolate and Snoopy dances to my first readers and critique partners: Tom Threadgill, Linda Glaz, April Strauch, Michele Hughes, Cheryl Martin, Jessica Nelson, Camille Eide, and Emily Hendrickson. I'm in awe that God has given me the likes of you to help me string words together with succinct and pithy flair. Tom and Linda, I owe you extra chocolate and you know why. Tom, please thank your beautiful wife, Janet, for me, for sharing your time with this book!

To my prayer buddies, author Kate Breslin and author Kathy Rouser, I can't thank you enough for seeing me to the finish line.

I thank my heavenly Father and his Son, Jesus Christ, for hearing my cry each day as I write. He is a very present help. Thank you, Lord, for your precious Holy Spirit who guides with such gentle wisdom.

As for any good this book may do, the glory belongs to him alone.

Introduction

*People were also bringing babies to Jesus
for him to place his hands on them.*
—LUKE 18:15

Christmas 1998
Bentonville, Arkansas

Where were they?

I scanned the children on the stage, eager to spot Isaac and Isaiah in the matching outfits I'd dressed them in for the Christmas program. I hoped their new shoes didn't bother them too much. They hated shoes.

One by one I checked each precious face, searching for my babies, but they weren't there. I checked again, certain I'd missed them in the confusion of teachers lining children up like living dolls—side by side—across the front of the enormous stage.

But there was no set of twins on the stage with matching outfits and brand new shoes. No crooked little smiles and droopy eyelids. No identical miniature boys with botched haircuts (because of their incessant wiggling) that helped others tell them apart.

My neck felt hot and tears pushed against the corners of my eyes. I stood and walked the long aisle to the back doors, a definite no-no for a well-mannered pastor's wife. I couldn't sit for one more nanosecond.

I had to find them.

Jo, one of my friends who often helped me with the twins, met me in the hall.

"I knew you'd be out here," Jo said.

"What's going on? Where are they?" By this time I couldn't hold back the tears. Hurt and disappointment mixed with fear, creating a heavy pounding in my chest.

Jo blocked my way. "The teachers thought it best if they didn't participate. I knew you'd be upset, but there was nothing I could do."

"So, where are they?"

"In a room with David."

David? The janitor?

I ran to the education area of the building with Jo at my high heels and found David staring at my confused, raging little boys banging their heads against the wall.

"What's going on?"

I ran to the boys and took them in my arms.

The janitor shrugged. "I don't know. I was told to watch them."

"Jo, please help me find their shoes. We're going home."

I did my best to calm them, but they would not be consoled. It was too much. We had failed them. All of us. Me and their new outfits, the church, and their inexperienced teachers. I stuffed their shoes in my bag.

"C'mon, sweethearts. Let's go."

Jo picked up Isaiah and I scooped up Isaac. Together, we carried them screaming through the halls of the church.

A few weeks later in a private meeting with the head pastor, he shared some of his observations and concerns about the boys and then asked me something I'd never thought of before.

"Do you think you missed the will of God when you adopted them?"

I was stunned.

Did I? How was I to know? Were they not as worthy of love as anyone else?

My husband looked at me and I cleared my throat. Standing to leave, I said, "If I did, it doesn't matter now, does it?"

That meeting reminded me of others who had warned me not to take this journey:

"You already have a ministry."

"You'll never have a successful singing ministry now."

"You should think of all the other people who need you. Let someone else do this."

"When you found out they were damaged, why didn't you give them back?"

I'm glad I didn't listen to them. It's been a difficult, challenging journey, and I'm the first to admit I've made mistakes along the way. I'm far from a perfect parent and advocate. But I do not regret for one moment being what Isaiah says I am: their Motherbird.

Chapter 1

The Call

Here I am; you called me.
—1 SAMUEL 3:6

I peeked into the car seat for the fifth time to see if he was real.

"I can't believe they're letting us drive away." I glanced out the back window. No one followed us. We were thoroughly alone with a brand-new human in tow. "They just handed him to us and here we are. I'm the first mom he's ever known."

My husband, Eddie, glanced at the rearview mirror. "I keep thinking someone is going to stop us."

No one did.

The squirming little package snuggled deep in his car seat was safe—at least for now—from the frosty Iowa night and an uncertain future.

"Just in time for Christmas." I sighed. "What a happy Christmas this will be."

"He's twice as small as our boys when they were born." Eddie chuckled.

I nodded, remembering how fat and healthy our eight-pound sons had appeared when they came screaming into the world. This little fellow weighed just over five pounds and he practically disappeared in the soft blue sleeper I'd bought him.

Infertility issues brought us to foster care, and our love for children kept us hoping to make a difference in young lives. We initially became licensed foster parents, thinking perhaps we wouldn't be blessed with another child. But God did indeed bless us with a second son, and after moving to a new pastorate, we kept our foster license active.

"I'm already in love with him. It will be difficult to let him go when the time comes." I fussed with the blanket framing his face.

Eddie nodded. "He's a beautiful baby."

As an abandoned child myself, I kept a permanent corner of my heart for foster children and needy kids everywhere. My dream was to feed and comfort them all. I wanted them to know they were planned for and loved by God. I ached for hurting kids.

Eddie turned down the radio and glanced back at us. "What shall we name him?"

"Can you believe we get to give this tiny angel his first name?" I stared out the window at the stars in the black November sky. "How about Gabriel?"

"I like it. It's strong."

I looked down at the tiny bundle sleeping without a care. "What do you think, little cherub? You like it too?"

A Family for Gabriel

We were only supposed to have Gabriel for six weeks. Three months later the phone rang.

"Mrs. Akins, it's Carol from Lutheran Social Services. Do you have a minute?"

"Sure. What's up?"

"Due to Gabriel's background, we're having a difficult time placing him. Because we don't know his developmental potential and the circumstances surrounding his birth, we—"

"Then why can't we keep him? I mean, he's three months old already."

"I wish that were an option, but our agency's policy is that we only adopt to childless couples."

"That's not fair."

There was silence on the phone. "No, it's not. I'm sorry."

I looked at Gabriel, smiling up at me from his bouncy seat. I was his mother. He was my son. How much longer before they took him?

It was too easy for me to grow attached: the night feedings, the smiles at changing time, the way he grabbed onto my hair. I was completely in love with that little man. And if there was one thing I wanted him to know, it was that he was wanted. He was loved. He had a purpose.

I kept a diary for him:

Dear Gabriel,

Today you reached for me and my heart melted. How very precious you are to me. You are such a dear, sweet baby. You cuddle up with no fear of tomorrow. You're secure in your little bed as you sleep next to Mama and Daddy each night. Oh, how very much we love you. But I know that one day, I'll not be able to hold you in my arms because you belong to someone else. I wish it wasn't so. I even pray it isn't so. But I want God's perfect will for your life, dear one. I want you to grow wise and strong, and for you to fulfill the purpose God has for your life. How very precious you are to me, but how much more precious you are to God.

Love, Mama

Six months grew into nine months. Eddie and I filed papers with the state of Iowa to adopt. We submitted to a home study and revealed every single wart and skeleton of our lives. If no one was willing to adopt Gabriel, we were. We loved him as our own.

I prayed constantly.

"Dear God, please give him to us if it's your perfect will. If not, please help me to let him go. But you should know, I don't want him to leave. I want to keep him. Please, if there's any way at all, please let him stay."

Months went by and as he grew, we were hopeful that God would allow us to adopt this beautiful boy. He loved playing peekaboo with our youngest, Noah, and laughing at our older son, Jesse. He adored our daughter, Melissa, and squealed when she walked into the room.

"Mama."

He called me Mama!

When he was nearly eleven months old, the phone rang.

It was Carol from Lutheran Social Services.

"This is hard, Karla, and I have strong mixed feelings. We've found a family for Gabriel."

I couldn't speak. My eyes welled up with tears.

What do you mean you found a family?

He already has a family.

And just like that, with one day's notice, he was no longer ours. He belonged to Them. Those I Did Not Know. And I would never see him again. He would call someone else Mama and she would watch him take his first steps, learn his ABCs, and graduate from high school.

The next day I dressed him in his cutest outfit and packed all his clothes, except for the outfit I found him in at the hospital, his ID bracelet, and a pair of shoes. I sent his diary and a note to his new parents about all his favorite things: steamed carrots, listening to music, strawberry ice cream.

I imagined how excited they must feel to finally have their own child. Something they undoubtedly had longed for and prayed for. I imagined his reaction to them and how he would delight them because he was a bubbly, happy baby, and he'd had much attention from siblings and church folks and wasn't afraid of strangers. I was certain they would fall in love with him immediately.

I couldn't carry him out to the social worker's car. I stood in the kitchen beside him in his car seat on the table and kissed his happy face with my tears. The little angel had no idea he'd never see me again—that he was going somewhere new and strange and wonderful. Finally, Eddie picked him up and walked him out to the car, and I could hear the tears in his voice as he spoke to the little fellow that he too had grown to love.

"You're getting a new mom and dad, Gabe. You're going to have a wonderful life."

The pain was the most excruciating I'd ever known.

It was worse than death because he was out there somewhere and I didn't know what he was feeling or if he was hungry or scared. I had to get away, to wrestle with these overwhelming emotions and cry out to God. He and I had business to take care of.

Wrestling with God

My friend Nancy, who is now with Jesus, had a family cottage on a lake. It wasn't fancy but it was a peaceful, comforting refuge. How I managed the hour drive I can't remember. But once inside the security of its walls, I cried as I'd never cried before.

"Is this what it's like to lose those you love, Lord? How many of your children never return?"

Over and over I cried, "Though you slay me, I will praise you."

In every room of the house, I shouted it aloud, thankful that it was off-season at the lake and no one was close enough to hear my gut-wrenching wails. It was a primal kind of crying I'd never experienced and hope I never will again.

Weeks later I got a picture of Gabriel and his new parents from the social worker. They were adorable. She was petite and pretty and he was extremely handsome with dark features. With Gabriel's dark brown eyes, he could easily pass for their own biological child.

I was happy for their joy, but felt as if God had chosen them over me because they were more worthy. "What's wrong with me, God, that you couldn't see fit for us to keep him? What do they have that we don't?"

Grief can skew your thinking. And I was confused, hurt, and not sure what to do with these overwhelming emotions.

But God knew.

And three months later?

We got the call.

Chapter 2

Sea of Grief

Blessed are those who mourn, for they will be comforted.
—MATTHEW 5:4

Those first minutes, days, and then weeks without Gabriel, I felt as if my head was detached from my body and I was watching myself from somewhere on the ceiling. I burst into tears at the slightest provocation.

"Mama, what's wrong?" Jesse and Noah asked in unison when they caught me crying in the basement laundry room.

"I forgot to put soap in the washing machine."

I'm glad I didn't know that this period of drowning was but a dress rehearsal for what would become a lifelong swim in troubled waters. The sorrow we'd experience as we learned to navigate the crashing waves of the twins' disabilities threatened to envelop our happy home with dark, heavy storm clouds.

The Call

One afternoon as I was helping our children with a history lesson, the cordless phone on my desk rang.

"Hi, Karla, it's Jenny. Listen, we have preemie twin boys at the NICU at Blank Children's Hospital in Des Moines who need a home. I was wondering if you and your husband could head down there for an infant CPR class because one of them is ready to be released today."

"Uh, can I talk to Eddie and call you back?"

"How long do you think that will take?"

I was surprised by her impatience. "Give us thirty minutes?"

"Fine. I'll be waiting for your call."

I called my husband, who was in the church office a block away, and asked him to come home. We sat the children down and talked to them.

"Remember how the Bible talks about taking care of orphans and widows? And that if we help them it's like taking care of Jesus?"

The kids nodded. But they were afraid too. They didn't want to lose these babies the way we lost Gabriel.

As a family, we prayed and decided to tell the social worker yes. We would take it a day at a time.

"I'm glad," she said. "I'd already put your name on the court order."

Isaiah came home first. There was nothing romantic about our first interactions with him. As soon as I dressed him in his going-home outfit, he promptly threw up all over it. That should have been my first clue. Life with these little ones would be fraught with challenges.

Eddie taught at a Bible college in Des Moines, ninety miles from our house. After classes, he stopped at the hospital to rock and pray over Isaac for the month he remained in the hospital. I called every day to check on him and ask how he behaved compared to his twin.

These babies cried and screamed—a lot. I knew something wasn't right about them but assumed it was because they were premature. They didn't cuddle up like my other infants did. Instead, they arched their backs and fought being fed. The only way to feed them was to swaddle them tightly and tug gently on the tiny bottle to help them remember to suck, swallow, and breathe. Sometimes they'd forget to breathe and we had to remove the bottle and let them catch their breath before continuing. It took an hour for them to empty their tiny two-ounce bottle and they had to eat every two hours.

This wasn't the happy experience I'd hoped for when signing up to adopt. I had no idea of the neurological damage they had as a result of being born to a mother who drank alcohol.

"Mama, my ears hurt when they scream." Jesse didn't like the constant crying. No one did.

"Yes, I know." I held him next to me on the couch. "Maybe it's because they are so little and their tummies hurt."

Months later we learned that the boys were on the fetal alcohol disorder spectrum. When a pregnant mother drinks, the alcohol enters her bloodstream and crosses the placenta. The baby metabolizes alcohol slower than the mother and the alcohol concentration in their blood is much higher than in hers. Because this interferes with the delivery of oxygen and optimal nutrition to the baby's developing brain, there are devastating consequences for the child. Impairment of the central nervous system, facial features, bones, and heart may occur.

The screaming and crying were constant. They didn't interact, and in the early years they crawled about the floor howling and biting one another for no apparent reason. Their backs were covered in bite marks (they got their teeth early—at the age of three months). Soothing them was nearly impossible, except for when we took them for a ride in my daughter's noisy car. Meal times were a dreaded lesson in dodging flying bowls, sippy cups, and food.

At their first developmental checkup, their heads measured at the tenth percentile on the growth chart in comparison with the rest of their bodies.

The doctor entered the room and announced, "They're microcephalic."

I knew what she meant because I'd cared for foster children with microcephaly before. Their heads were too small. If their skulls didn't grow, their brains would be squished, and there would be dire consequences: seizures, severe cognitive development, even trouble walking.

Shock does strange things to a person. When the doctor told me, I pictured dinosaurs. They had small brains but they seemed to get along just fine. I remember looking the doctor in the eye and saying so.

"Well, yes," she said. "But dinosaurs' brains didn't have pressure on them."

Tears spilled from my eyes as I looked into their little faces. I felt like the walls were closing in. I couldn't get out of the exam room fast enough.

Those first four years we traveled blindly from doctor to doctor with unanswered questions. The twins' heads were growing properly so the tantrums, terror, and self-injurious behaviors were a mystery to me. One of their developmental pediatricians told me that I wasn't spending enough one-on-one time with the twins and that was why they were so difficult.

I had been a mother long enough to know they were not developing in a typical way. They didn't play like other children and showed no interest in make-believe. They didn't talk and potty training was out of the question. They had no concept of what a bathroom was for.

When we moved from Iowa to Arkansas, we enrolled the twins in a developmental preschool. It was there that we started our journey toward learning what was truly going on with the boys and about a condition I'd never had any experience with before.

Autism.

It's hard for me to imagine now that I knew so little about autism. But it was 1998 and the disease wasn't as prevalent back then, while today one in fifty-four boys are affected. Well-known organizations, such as Autism Speaks, hadn't been founded yet, and the only information I could get my hands on came from brochures at doctors' offices. Reliable, results-proven therapies, such as Applied Behavior Analysis (ABA), were just beginning to surface.

Stages of Grief and Grace

As the twins grew and failed to reach normal milestones, the grief was often debilitating. I remember apologizing to my husband for my desire to adopt these little boys, but he never wavered or expressed any regrets. I was grateful for the anchor I had in him because I worried about the effect the constant screaming had on our relationship and our other children. Sometimes I wondered if our family would survive the stress.

Grieving is a natural reaction to learning about a child's disability. And it comes and goes throughout the child's life because a parent can't help but wonder "what might have been." You may find yourself in different stages of grief at various and unexpected times. I experienced each stage in startling ways, but now I look at them as precious times of molding by God's hands as I learned to rest in his grace.

Denial and Isolation

I didn't stay in this stage long because I knew something was wrong. But I did isolate myself in some ways. Often, the isolation wasn't entirely my fault. Most of my friends didn't understand what I was going through. But in their defense, I didn't exactly spell it out either. I didn't want them to think I was sorry for adopting the twins. I didn't want anyone to know how hard it was because I feared their judgment. In hindsight, I wish I had reached out more for help in those dark times.

Anger

Sometimes anger would manifest itself in strange ways and at the wrong times or things. I couldn't control autism. I couldn't fix it. My anger toward autism would manifest by my anger at things that weren't significant. I'd find myself furious with other things I might be able to control, such as a rude medical professional or social worker or an ignorant teacher. I was angry at the laws, angry at the medical community, angry at anyone who glared at me at the grocery store because the boys were so loud. Finally, I had to admit that what I was really angry about was why God allowed children to suffer. Why had he put adoption in my heart only to have it turn out so difficult?

Bargaining with God

I don't remember bargaining with God in terms of, "God if you do this, I'll do this." But I did ask (and still find myself asking at times), "Why?" A lot. Logically, I realize that God has no obligation to tell me why. But my heart longs to know.

When working with the most severe cases of autism—or any disability, really—I find myself wondering about God's ways. That's a legitimate question and one that doesn't offend God. As long as we ask our questions while humbly recognizing that our finite minds can't understand an infinite God, our Lord can handle our doubts about his plans: "'For my thoughts are not your thoughts, neither are your ways my ways,' declares the LORD. 'As the heavens are higher than the earth, so are my ways higher than your ways and my thoughts than your thoughts'" (Isa. 55:8–9).

I know the big answer to "why" is that we live in a fallen world with imperfect genes. I know that one day we will reign with him with perfect bodies and there will be no more pain or tears. I look forward to that day. As I work as a court-appointed special advocate and visit children's homes where children live their entire lives in the confines of a bed, I get angry at the pain and sorrow that reigns on this earth. But this isn't all there is. My focus remains on the One who will rescue us from all this distress. I look forward to a pain-free eternity of hanging out with my boys and other children as we reign with Jesus in perfect bodies and minds. It's going to be awesome.

Depression

This is probably the longest and most common stage of them all. At least for me it was (and is). It's easy to find yourself focusing on what you don't have or what you're missing out on. The simple stress of living with autism can cause the brain to go into fight-or-flight mode. According to the *Journal of Autism and Developmental Disorders*, mothers of children with autism experience levels of chronic stress similar to those of combat soldiers.[1] Chronic stress by itself can develop into depression. When coupled with grief over a child's diagnosis, this puts parents of children with autism at great risk for depression. Feelings of helplessness can be overwhelming. Learning to cope with the stress and focusing on the positives, including God's love, are essential for getting past this stage of grief.

Acceptance

Accepting my boys' diagnoses wasn't hard. What was hard for me was accepting that I couldn't fix it. It was the strangest realization. When my

other children were sick, I could fix the situation by giving them medicine. I fixed their pain with love and Band-Aids. But I couldn't fix the
twins. When I finally surrendered them to the Lord, I was able to move
through this stage of grief in victory. It's not easy by any means. I still
have to do this day to day as they continue to experience challenges as
adults. Accepting and embracing this journey with autism made it more
of an adventure than a tragedy. God's providence can be trusted. Trusting
that God has a plan is a huge piece of the acceptance puzzle. And if there's
one thing I do know, you can trust him even when nothing makes sense.

Moving On

There comes a time when the grieving is shelved and the fight begins.
Without prayer, time alone with the Lord, and the compassion of friends,
I couldn't have survived. It's been twenty-two years now, and the grief
still comes and goes, but in different ways. There are some constant things
that help me deal with my grief. As you search for a lifeline in the sea of
despair, consider reaching for some of these supports.

Be Kind to Yourself

You are not a failure. See yourself as God sees you: highly favored and
blessed. When God looks at you, he sees his beloved Son, Jesus. When Jesus
paid for your sins on the cross, he took all your shame, guilt, and condemnation. Romans 5:20 tells us that where sin abounds, God's grace abounds
all the more. When God looks at you, a Christian, he only sees the perfection of his Son. He doesn't see your bad attitude or self-pity or any other
unseemly behavior you may exhibit due to stress. Your self-proclaimed fail-
ures are not who you are. You are God's sons and daughters (2 Cor. 6:18).
Oh, how very much he loves you! That alone is reason to rejoice!

Do Something to Comfort Yourself

Take a long walk or bubble bath. Go to a bookstore or library and spend
the day alone reading. Your idea of comforting yourself can be completely
different from anything I suggest. Find what refuels you and helps you
to think straight about life, God, and his amazing love for you. He is the

Wonderful Counselor and the Prince of Peace (Isa. 9:6). In him you will find rest and comfort.

Be Keenly Aware That You Are Not Alone

Psalm 34:18 says, "The Lord is close to the brokenhearted and saves those who are crushed in spirit." Never, ever believe the lie that you are doing this autism journey by yourself. Tap into the presence of God. He is there for you. "Then you will call on me and come and pray to me, and I will listen to you. You will seek me and find me when you seek me with all your heart. I will be found by you" (Jer. 29:12–14).

Memorize a Scripture Passage

Repeat it over and over until you get past the pain or stressful moment. My repeated mantra is, "Praise the LORD; for his mercy endureth for ever" (2 Chron. 20:21 KJV). I repeat this or other memorized Scriptures when I'm afraid, when I'm frustrated, or when I'm simply out of words to pray. The stress level is so high at times that it helps to have these words on your lips. It keeps them speaking life.

Make Up New Songs About Your Situation

You don't have to be a musician or a great singer to do this. Sing praises to him while you bathe your fussy child (my twins hate showers and baths) or drive a screaming child to the doctor's office. King David set a great example for us to follow. While he tended his sheep, he spent time praising the Lord. While you tend to your little lamb, you can do the same. "Sing to the LORD a new song; sing to the LORD, all the earth" (Ps. 96:1).

Get Alone to Yell, Cry, Stomp Your Feet, and Wrestle with God

Is it wrong to mourn or be angry? Absolutely not. In fact, to say so would suggest that God is unable to handle it or get us through it. He's not surprised by your feelings. He is all-knowing. Hiding and denying them will do you no good. You'll feel better after unloading your troubles. God has big shoulders. Psalm 62:8 says, "Trust in him at all times, you people; pour out your hearts to him, for God is our refuge."

Pray for God's Grace

If I succeed, it's not by my own power but by God's grace (Zech. 4:6). When I'm at the end of myself, feeling frustrated and alone, his grace gives me the strength to take the next step and face a new day. I pray for grace constantly. His grace transcends my normal limits of endurance, patience, and self-control. I don't have it within me to exhibit these fruits of the Spirit by myself. "But he said to me, 'My grace is sufficient for you, for my power is made perfect in weakness.' Therefore I will boast all the more gladly about my weaknesses, so that Christ's power may rest on me" (2 Cor. 12:9).

Accept God's Plan for Your Child and Your Family

Remind yourself that God is up to something good. You can trust him even when nothing makes sense. Don't live by what you feel. Live by the authority of God's Word. He promises that he will never leave us (Matt. 28:20) and that he hears us when we pray. Psalm 103:19 reminds us that God is in control: "The LORD has established his throne in heaven, and his kingdom rules over all." And later in the Psalms, one of my favorite Scripture passages reminds us there is nowhere we can go that God is not there with us: "Where can I go from your Spirit? Where can I flee from your presence? If I go up to the heavens, you are there; if I make my bed in the depths, you are there. If I rise on the wings of the dawn, if I settle on the far side of the sea, even there your hand will guide me, your right hand will hold me fast" (Ps. 139:7–10).

Depending on what stage of grief you are in, some of these suggestions may not apply. Be patient with yourself. In time, you may travel through all the stages of grief. You may revisit each stage more than once. I certainly do.

But the most important thing I want you to know is this: you and your children are loved far beyond what you could ever imagine.

God wants you to know this too.

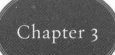

Chapter 3

God Is Up to Something Good

"Though the mountains be shaken and the hills be
removed, yet my unfailing love for you will not be shaken
nor my covenant of peace be removed," says the LORD, *who*
has compassion on you.

—ISAIAH 54:10

I love animals. I have three dogs and two cats. If I could, I'd have a zoo. But I live in a small community that doesn't allow in-town residents to own a wildlife refuge. My husband wouldn't allow such a menagerie either. (He likes animals, but I border on obsessed.)

I'm enthralled with God's imagination. He has amazing ideas, right down to the frogs and toads in and around my pond that pierce the nighttime quiet with their deafening croaks of springtime joy. While other folks are annoyed by these noisy critters, I find great delight in knowing their Creator designed them for a purpose. They sing exactly as he created them. These wonders give me an incredibly secure feeling: God has a plan, even for noisy little amphibians.

When I'm in a particularly joyful mood, you might hear me blurt out praises about creation: "God, thank you for trees. Trees are such a great idea. I'm glad you thought of them. I think it's really cool how deep their roots grow and how strong they stand against the wind. I love how they give me shade in the summer and how pretty their leaves are in the fall. How did you ever think of that? Clever you."

While one day I'm in awe of a tree, the next day I may praise him for my little pug dog snuggling next to me while I write (as he's doing now): "God, thank you for little pugs that snore. Dogs are such a great idea. Thanks for creating an animal that would be a good friend to humans."

God Is Good

My worldview is such that God is good. I don't believe he makes mistakes. He has a purpose for every living creature and thing. I believe he created the heavens and the earth perfectly, but when the humans he placed in this perfect world disobeyed him, the imperfections of sickness, diseases, and hatefulness interrupted his perfect plan and world.

It's pretty simple in my mind: God = good; Satan = bad.

It's also a matter of perception. What one person sees as a burden may actually be a blessing. Maybe not in its rawest form, but I truly believe that God is always up to something good. We only see a tiny part of the picture.

It's easy to understand what a small part of that picture we see after we've gone for a plane ride. As the plane takes off, the buildings and people on the ground grow smaller and smaller. We can see much more of the big picture when we're up high. The closer we get to the ground, the less we can see. We perceive only those things that are right in front of us.

I think eternity is something like this. God sees each part of the puzzle. He knows where all the pieces fit. We may not see what part of the puzzle autism is in the grand scheme of things, but he can. There is a purpose for having autism in our lives. And while the enemy may have tried to discourage us with this condition, God is up to something good.

The story of Joseph (Gen. 37–50) encourages me greatly in this journey of parenting. His biography reminds me that life is extremely unfair, but in that unfairness God is in control. I marvel at Joseph's wisdom and his forgiveness toward the brothers who sold him away as a slave. During this enslavement, he was falsely accused of rape and placed in prison for years. But God brought him out of prison and promoted him to governor—the second highest position in Egypt. Because of these circumstances, Joseph saved his family from starving. My favorite part of this story is his response to the brothers who sold him: "You intended to harm me, but God intended it for good to accomplish what is now being done, the saving of many lives" (Gen. 50:20).

Joseph accepted his path in life because he knew that God had a plan. God's designs are always better than our own. If we unselfishly follow his road map, he will make something beautiful out of the barricades and detours.

I don't claim to understand why autism is in my life or anyone else's. I certainly never expected to be the mother of children with such a violent, life-altering diagnosis. But I do know that God has blessed us in beautiful ways and faithfully provided help when we needed it. I've learned more about myself and life by living with autism than I would have otherwise. I rejoice over things I never celebrated before. I find immense joy in the twins' enthusiasm over small things. My sense of humor is wackier and my level of patience for life's annoyances much greater.

I remember standing in line at the grocery store some time ago, listening to a woman complain about how long the checker took to ring items through. I smiled to myself thinking, "At least you're not standing in line with twins with autism throwing things out of the cart, lady. Try dealing with that and you'll realize waiting for a slow checker is a piece of cake."

I had a neighbor once who vacuumed her carpeted garage daily and complained about the leaves in my yard because a few (very few) blew across the road onto her property. Personally, I'm a live-and-let-live sort of person. I grew up in southern Kansas where the trees are few and the leaves are pretty much crispy wisps of nothing by the end of summer. I didn't grow up raking leaves, but I did grow up raking prairie grass.

When the twins were small, raking leaves wasn't on my to-do list, not only because I didn't think of it but also because, even if I did, I didn't have the time or energy. In the whole scheme of my challenging life, a few little leaves from my one pitiful tree didn't rank at the top of my priorities. I used to think resentfully, "What that lady needs is a couple of kids with autism. Then she wouldn't have time to vacuum her garage and judge my leaves."

I now realize I'm the blessed one. I'm the one who experiences the miracle of my sons' ability to feel compassion for others. I'm the one who was there the first time the boys called me "Mama" and said "I love you" at the age of seven. My fastidious neighbor didn't get to experience their excitement and pride in winning medals at the Special Olympics. All she had was a clean carpet in her garage.

I have so much more.

God Always Acts for the Best

Is God up to something good? You better believe it.

Nancy Honeytree is a pioneer in Christian music and has long been one of my favorite musicians. I grew up singing her songs. We had the privilege of hosting her at our church some years ago, and when she introduced us to this song, the words changed my thinking forever. Now when I go through tough times, I sing and recite these words:

> I'm gonna believe, that You are up to something good
> When I can't understand, the things that happen in my life
> I'm gonna believe that You are up to something good.
> "I'll never fail or forsake you," that is what You said,
> "Through fire and water I'll take you,"
> That is what You said
> And when you don't answer my prayers the way I think You should,
> I'm gonna believe that You are up to something good![1]

The enemy of this world—Satan—is relentless. But not more so than God. While Satan intends to harm and destroy us, God is there with his perfect love that protects and shields us. He provided a way out from the wiles of the devil through the life of his Son, Jesus Christ.

As a Christian, I believe that Jesus, born of the Virgin Mary, is God's

Son. I believe God sent him to earth as a way for humans to restore a right relationship with their heavenly Father. Before the death of Christ, a great chasm of sin and death separated us from God. But when we accept Christ as our Savior, we're given the grace and permission to speak to God with boldness.

Why is knowing this important when dealing with autism? Because knowing that God is good and not bad, and that it's the enemy's goal to destroy us and our families, helps us know the proper way to pray and approach God. I believe that God grieves when we grieve. Our tears are not lost on him. He stores them and records and remembers them (Ps. 56:8). He does not ignore us and leave us without a helper. Even if we *feel* alone, as his precious children we simply are not.

God did not send autism into your life to punish you or your children. That is not the kind of God we serve. Our very good God allows things to happen to us for a purpose. And sometimes it's painful when he places us on his potter's wheel and shapes us into the people he plans for us to be. But if we can remain open to *his* ideas instead of our own, and listen for that still, small voice above the screams and tantrums, he can show us amazing ways to grow and cope on this autism journey.

I honestly don't know how anyone raises a child without the guidance of the Scriptures and daily prayer, much less a child with autism. If I didn't have the Lord to call upon in my dark, lonely moments of overwhelming distress, I don't know where I'd be today. It's knowing he is there for me day in and day out that keeps me putting one foot in front of the other. When the twins were younger and I woke up each morning to their feces rubbed on the walls and all over themselves, I needed a God bigger than my despair and frustration. I needed a grace that would build my faith because it's faith that moves his mighty hand.

He has great plans for you and your children. Everything that the enemy plans to use to destroy you, God will use for good and will help others. I'm sure autism isn't what you had planned, and that's a hard thing to accept. But I do believe that these unexpected detours can make us stronger if we let them. They will make us better, not bitter, if our hearts trust in God's good and perfect plan: "Do not be anxious about anything, but in every situation, by prayer and petition, with thanksgiving, present your requests to God. And the peace of God, which transcends all understanding, will guard your hearts and your minds in Christ Jesus" (Phil. 4:6–7).

Autism: it isn't *who* your child is. Autism is simply a name for a developmental disability that causes significant social, communication, and behavioral challenges. Your child is precious, planned for, and valuable to God. As much as you love your child, God loves them even more. He has a plan and a purpose for their life. He knows what they need.

God's Ways Are Not Our Ways

When we adopted the twins, several well-meaning folks were concerned that I was ruining a potential career in music. Some doors were opening for me at the time that could have meant singing on an international TV program. Besides that, we still had great responsibilities in ministry as my husband was a full-time head pastor.

We were criticized by several groups of our peers for taking on two little boys with so many special needs. One church leader said, "When you found out they were damaged, why didn't you give them back?"

Isn't it amazing what people let fly off their lips? *Give them back?* They aren't puppies I can take to the pound. I didn't get them at a supercenter where I can get a refund. Besides, I threw away the receipt. I had no intention of giving them back—ever! They are my boys. God ordained for them to be my boys. Does God give us away when we are less than perfect? I should say not! And thankfully so, or he'd have to give away the whole lot of us!

One afternoon during a minister's conference a preacher looked me in the eye and said, "You know, you'll never have a singing career now that you have these boys in your life." Another singer said, "If you weren't tied down with those boys, you'd be able to go on tour with me. Now you're stuck. For years."

Sometimes I wonder if God uses autism as a mirror. I can tell a lot about a person by the way they react to my sons. It's an immediate barometer of their character. That's not to say I should judge someone who is ignorant of the condition. Not at all. But autism has an accurate way of measuring a person's tolerance, don't you think?

I have no way of knowing if a singing career would have been in the bag or not. But what I do know is this: anyone who sings well can have a singing career if they want it. But only *I* could be these little boys' mother. God had orchestrated my life in a way that granted me the privilege of traveling down this road with them. Did I have moments of doubt? You better believe it. When I was elbow deep in messy diapers at home (and they were eight years old) and still wrestling with tantrums in public places, that singing career looked a lot greener than the pasture I was "stuck" in.

I say with full confidence today that I do not regret the road I chose in being mother to twins with autism. It's been a highway of potholes, broken bridges, and back alleys, but it's taken me places I'd never otherwise have traveled. I've learned more about human nature, kindness, and compassion. I'm more sensitive and caring than I would have been before. I know more about all sorts of things I wouldn't have known otherwise.

But it's not all about us. It's not even all about our children. It's all about God and his perfect plan. Believing that God has a perfect plan for your child may be difficult, especially if your son or daughter has a severe form of autism. But he doesn't allow anything to happen in this world without a purpose: "I make known the end from the beginning, from ancient times, what is still to come. I say, 'My purpose will stand, and I will do all that I please.' From the east I summon a bird of prey; from a far-off land, a man to fulfill my purpose. What I have said, that I will bring about; what I have planned, that I will do" (Isa. 46:10–11).

Keeping Truth on Our Lips
Yes, there is a good God with an excellent plan for us. We can confess these truths out loud each day over our situations with autism. If you don't

know what to confess, try reciting the following personalized prayers, which are based on Scripture, and allow them to build your faith:

- "Lord, I cry out to you in my trouble because you will bring me out of my distress. You, who still the storm to a whisper and hush the waves of the sea, can calm the storms in my heart when everything spins out of control." (See Ps. 107:28–30.)

- "Lord, you created my child(ren) and you know they have autism. It is no surprise to you when we feel frustrated and helpless. You make everything beautiful in its time. I can't comprehend what you will do from the beginning to the end of our lives, especially in the life of my child with autism. So, I trust you even when it doesn't make sense and the pieces don't fit because I know you see the beginning and the end." (See Eccl. 3:11.)

- "Lord, I have sown many tears over my child with autism. I now pray that you will show me the way to reap with songs of joy. Help me to trust that you are doing a new and wonderful thing in my life. You will make a way in this wilderness and rivers in this desert of autism. No matter what beasts I encounter, I will overcome them because your Word is truth. Thank you for going with me through the fire and flood and bringing me to a wealthy place in my life and in the life of my child with autism. Help me to recognize this wealthy place when I arrive." (See Ps. 126:5–6; Isa. 43:19–21; John 17:17; Ps. 66:12.)

- "Lord, help me to understand that there are things I see that are temporary things and there are things I cannot see that are eternal. Help me to remember to keep my eyes not on the raging sea around me, but upon you. And when I feel like drowning, please remind me to cry out to you in my distress as Peter did in the storm when he was sinking." (See 2 Cor. 4:18; Matt. 14:28–31.)

- "Lord, help me to remember that you are up to something good. As you had a plan for Joseph, you have a plan for me. Help me to have faith, even when I don't understand it, that you are in control and you have my best interest at heart. Help my unbelief, Lord. I am weak but you are strong. Help me to depend on that strength." (See Mark 9:23–25; 2 Cor. 12:9.)

As you speak God's Word aloud over your situations with autism, your faith will grow. You will feel stronger and have more awareness that you are not alone. Sometimes I pray when I don't feel like it, simply out of obedience, to get my mind in line with God's plan instead of my own.

He is faithful. He has never, ever not answered. And he will do the same for you. His Word declares that God does not show favoritism (Acts 10:34).

Remember Moses and the Hebrews when they faced the sea before them and the Egyptians behind them? The Israelites moaned and groaned and were afraid for their lives. They questioned Moses and God: "Why did you bring us here to die?" What did Moses say to them? "The LORD will fight for you; you need only to be still" (Exod. 14:14).

You need only to be still.

When you get into a cycle of questioning God because of autism, *be still*, and practice the faith to believe he is up to something good.

When you don't know which therapy to use, or whether the doctor's advice is the right choice for your child, *be still*, and wait for him to guide you and show you which way to go.

When you have been on the phone with insurance for five hours straight and still have no answers, *be still*, pray, and give the battle to the Lord.

When your child is out of control, you can be in control by *being still* and staying calm. Not easy, I know, but again, with him, you can.

This isn't a license to throw up your arms and be passive. Stillness is an action. By being still you are actively obeying him and listening for his voice. He has a plan. He's got this. He knows what's best and he will not fail to show you which way to go. He is fighting for you, not against you. He has your best interest at heart, and that means he has the best interest of your child at heart too.

God is fighting for you! Do you believe that? If you truly believe that, how can you be afraid? How can you worry?

Trust me, I'm no super-spiritual giant. I could not do this journey without God's grace. I hope you'll have the courage to trust him to help you. Praying won't instantly fix everything, but seeking God will make the journey less lonely and will strengthen you for the challenges you must face. He is there for you. Even if you don't think so or know so.

What do you have to lose if you call out to him today?

What do you have to lose if you don't?

Chapter 4

What Is Autism?

But he said to me, "My grace is sufficient for you, for my power is made perfect in weakness." Therefore I will boast all the more gladly about my weaknesses, so that Christ's power may rest on me.

—2 Corinthians 12:9

When the doctors first diagnosed my twin boys with autism in 1998, the only thing I knew about it was the character Dustin Hoffman played in the movie *Rain Man*. It sounds incredible, but I honestly wasn't aware that there was a diagnosis for people with developmental disabilities who acted as my boys did. Society was just beginning to be more aware of a growing group of behavioral characteristics called *autism*. Looking back on people I knew growing up, I can now understand that they may have had autism, when I thought they were intellectually disabled. I didn't understand that just because someone couldn't express themselves, it didn't mean they weren't intelligent.

Defining Autism

When my boys turned two, I realized that something wasn't "right" with them. They spent most of their time biting themselves and each other,

screaming, and hitting me. They didn't play with toys and were just learning to walk. They didn't babble and only cried. It was a constant guessing
game trying to figure out what they wanted. They were simply miserable.

So was I.

All I had at my fingertips for support was a rickety, 1980s-era IBM personal computer. As a pastor's wife, isolation was an issue for me. Because
of my husband's church position, I couldn't openly share what we were
going through as a family (I'll share more about that later).

That's how I wound up in an AOL autism chat room, filled to the
brim with mamas and grandmas who had children with autism. In those
days, proper citizens didn't post selfies and Facebook was nonexistent.
(Founder Mark Zuckerberg was then only thirteen years old.) Most people protected their privacy, so it was easy to remain anonymous. I spent
hours every evening sharing my struggles and reading about others who
fought the same battles. It was truly a blessing from the Lord to make
these new friends. I don't know how I would have managed otherwise.

What I learned from my desperate search for answers is that autism
was, and continues to be, a complex condition not easily understood by
researchers. Even though they had gathered and studied data, it was frag-
mented. There were (and continue to be) as many disagreements on how
to interpret the data as there were ideas about how to treat it.

Since the twins were born in 1995, technology has advanced from
landlines to cell phones and wireless computing. NASA has landed a rover
on Mars. We've seen the invention of the artificial heart, YouTube, and
iPads. You'd think there would be more progress regarding how science
perceives autism, but there isn't. Experts are still puzzled about the disorder, and there are no one-size-fits-all answers.

However, the signs to look for in a young child have remained consistent. According to the United States Centers for Disease Control,[1] a
toddler with Autism Spectrum Disorder (ASD) might do the following:

- Not look at what a parent points to
- Not notice or point to unusual objects, such as an airplane overhead

- Avoid eye contact
- Play alone
- Not be aware when people talk to them
- Repeat or echo words instead of answering questions appropriately
- Repeat actions over and over again
- Have trouble with transitions
- Be oversensitive to smells, tastes, textures, or water that touches the skin
- Lose skills they once had (such as language)
- Not play "pretend" games, such as feeding a doll or playing house
- Prefer not to be cuddled or held, except on their own terms

If your child or grandchild has any of these symptoms, I urge you to make an appointment with your child's pediatrician and ask for a referral to a developmental pediatrician or developmental psychiatrist. The earlier your child begins appropriate therapies, the better the chance of "rewiring" their brain.

A Neurological Condition

People with autism vary in IQ. They are not all cognitively impaired. In fact, some have quite high IQs. Autism has nothing to do with intelligence. It is a brain-based, neurological condition. It has less to do with psychology and more to do with biology. It is not a mental illness. It is a developmental disability that appears during the first three years of life, is five times more prevalent in boys than in girls, and respects no racial, ethnic, or social boundaries. Family income, lifestyle, and education have no effect on its occurrence.

Autism is often referred to as an "invisible disease" because you can't see autism by just looking at a person. But if you watch someone with autism, you may see that they interact, behave, and learn differently than most people. This spectrum is extremely broad and ranges from those with giftedness to the severely challenged. Some adults with autism can live independently, while others need constant supervision and support.

This brain disorder affects a person's ability to communicate, reason, and interact with others. The fact that it's a spectrum disorder makes it even more difficult to treat and understand because it affects individuals differently and to varying degrees of severity. As with my adopted twins—who were also diagnosed with fetal alcohol disorder, apraxia (an inability to manage coordinated movements, including their speech), and intellectual disability—autism is often found in combination with other disabilities.

A diagnosis of autism now includes several conditions that used to be diagnosed separately: autistic disorder, pervasive developmental disorder not otherwise specified (PDD-NOS), and Asperger's syndrome. These conditions are now all called autism spectrum disorder (ASD).

Today, according to the *Diagnostic and Statistical Manual of Mental Disorders*,[2] there are three levels of severity of autism.

Level Three
People at this level require very substantial support and have severe deficits in verbal and nonverbal communications that cause severe impairments in functioning. They are very limited in their initiations of social interactions and do not respond to social overtures from others. For example, they may have few words of intelligible speech and approach others in unusual ways in order to meet a need. Behaviorally, they are extremely inflexible and have great difficulty coping with change. They may exhibit repetitive behaviors that interfere with daily functioning.

When the twins were first diagnosed, they were at level three. It was a dark, scary time for us. Instead of interacting with us, they hit us. They hit strangers. They hit people at church and rarely, if ever, responded to their names. They cried and banged their heads on their cribs, on the walls, and on the cement sidewalk. They bit themselves and each other (and me). They refused to be comforted. Even if they were hungry, they threw their food back at me. It was utterly exhausting. I'd never felt so alone.

It was an angry time for me as well. Where was the support? Why were we required to do this alone? Who was there to call? Who would believe me? I'd never seen children act this way. I knew something was wrong, but even the doctors felt I simply had fussy babies in need of more one-on-one attention.

Level Two
People at this level require substantial support. Though they have marked deficits in verbal and nonverbal communication skills, they do speak. Even with support, their social interactions are limited because they don't initiate them on their own. When they respond to others, they often do so with odd verbal and nonverbal communication. Their interactions with others may focus on narrow special interests. They also have difficulty coping with change and transitions and exhibit repetitive or restricted behaviors enough to be noticed by others and to interfere with day-to-day functioning.

I have a friend whose teen son has Asperger's and a very high IQ. However, he only interacts with others regarding his own interests, which include his obsession with *Duck Dynasty* and *Larry the Cable Guy*. In interacting, he mostly repeats jokes he's heard from these characters instead of holding a typical, give-and-take conversation. Even though he is a brilliant student, his mother still has to guide him through his shower and all other daily living skills. He has to be eased into every transition and is very ritualistic regarding food. He sometimes is oppositional to the point of unreasonable rages. Because of his regimented behavior and lack of functional living skills, this young man probably falls into the level two category.

Another friend's highly intelligent teen son is regimented in his weekly activities and went through a period of obsessing about red purses, watching YouTube videos to learn how to make balloon sculptures, and making cupcakes. He also falls into level two because of a lack of self-help skills and the ability to care for himself independently.

My twins have intellectual disabilities. They fall into this category because of their inability to transition, speak, and interact appropriately with other people. As I've stated earlier, autism is no respecter of IQs. It is not a mental problem but a developmental disability.

Level One
People at this level require support because they have difficulty with social interactions. Their language may be stilted and unusual, and their attempts to make friends are typically unsuccessful. They have trouble switching activities, and their struggle to plan or organize their environment and schedule hampers their independence. They use language but may be difficult to understand. They may have difficulty understanding how to answer "wh" questions—who, what, when, where, and why.

The twins sometimes have a difficult time answering me when I ask, "What should I do after the clothes are finished in the washer?" Or, "What did you do today? Why did you do it?" They smile at me sweetly and lean their heads on my shoulder. That's their way of telling me, "I don't know how to answer you, but I'd like to."

All Levels of Functioning
People with autism usually have difficulty with verbal and nonverbal communication, social interactions, relationships, and casual activities such as play or recreation. They resist change in routines at all levels of functioning. Some may exhibit repeated body movements, such as hand flapping or rocking, and have unusual responses to objects. When my guys were little, it was toy emergency vehicles. For my friend's son, PJ, it was red purses.

In some cases, aggressive behavior may be present. Without medical treatment, both of my boys are aggressive. I'm grateful for the medication that has given them the ability to calm down and function without these behaviors. However, under certain circumstances, they can still exhibit these when frustrated. How many mothers are raising strong young men with autism without proper support? More than I care to think about. Conservatively, nearly 1.7 million people in the United States have a form of autism. The funding simply isn't there.

As a community, we need to do better.

Early Intervention Is Crucial

As I write this book, a recent study published by the *New England Journal of Medicine* reinforced the importance of early intervention. Comparing postmortem brain tissue of typical children and of children with autism revealed abnormalities in 90 percent of the children with autism, compared with about 10 percent of those without. The abnormalities were in the parts of the brain involved in social and emotional communication and language.[3]

The infant brain has a chance to rewire itself to compensate. That's why some parents of toddlers with autism who have pursued early intervention claim their child is "cured." Whether or not it's a cure in the scientific sense is not for me to say. But there is no doubt that early intervention is crucial for children with autism to have the best chance of making progress. The sooner a child can be meaningfully engaged, the better.

The difference in whether or not a child with autism will grow up to live on their own depends a lot on early interventions and the disorder's impact on the individual. Research shows that the earlier a child is diagnosed, the better the long-term effects of treatment. But autism is as unique to each person as a fingerprint. A therapy that is successful for one child may not register the same results with another child.

Isaac and Isaiah exhibit autism uniquely. One is more aggressive than the other. One displays repetitive speech—such as spelling out people's names instead of saying them—and the other doesn't. Even in these boys who are extremely alike physically, autism exhibits itself uniquely. Therefore, any of their successes that I write about in this book won't necessarily work in the same ways for others.

If you work in and around autism circles very long, you'll soon learn that there's an unfortunate divide regarding treatments, therapies, and even labels. Perhaps this is one reason autism research continues to fail to benefit families in their day-to-day struggles. More research and awareness must be done regarding the education and parenting of those with autism. Thousands of children with autism are growing up and becoming adults. Because these adults were not treated while young, more money has to be spent on day-to-day care for the rest of their lives. If the money had been spent on early intervention and family support, governments could have saved billions of dollars. The system is upside down.

As of this writing:

- One in sixty-eight children have autism (one in forty-two boys).[4]
- A two-decade long study by the state of California that concluded in 2007 showed that autism is the fastest-growing developmental disability, with a 1,148 percent growth rate.[5]
- Nearly 75 percent of costs are for adult services, but the costs of life-long care could be reduced by two-thirds with early diagnosis and intervention. Currently in the United States, the cost of autism over a life span is $2.4 million.[6]

It's frustrating to see money poured into research that doesn't bear fruit while young children with autism go without therapy and interventions that could improve their quality of life. Our public schools in the United States are sorely inadequate and behind in helping families with autism. Disability laws do not require a school to offer the latest innovative interventions. All that is required is that they "educate" the child in the "least restrictive environment."

It's not a matter of whether or not people with autism can learn. It's whether or not the adults in their lives can and will teach them. In my mind, it borders on child neglect and abuse when a society fails to throw a lifeline to these helpless youngsters when they need it most. In the United States today, only the rich can access the therapies and interventions that help young kids with autism become fully functioning adults.

The Best Interventions Are Free

Research-based and proven interventions are indeed expensive, but the best interventions are free. Nothing can replace a parent's time and love. I truly believe that the time my husband and I invested in spending time with the twins is what brought them the most progress. Spending time outdoors enjoying nature; learning the names of birds, trees, and plants; working in the yard; helping with chores; spending time cooking and cleaning—these are the things that helped the twins the most. No, we didn't have the fanciest schools or therapies. We only had faith to believe that God didn't give us little lambs without the pasture to put them in.

"With God all things are possible" (Matt. 19:26).

I clung to that Scripture verse and believed it the entire time my twins were growing up, and I continue to hold on to it today. Things I thought they may never do, they've done—more than I ever imagined.

God's Word tells us that we can't begin to imagine what he has in store for us (1 Cor. 2:9). I can testify to this.

I can hardly wait to tell you all about it.

Chapter 5

Autism Goes to School

*But the wisdom that comes from heaven is first of all pure;
then peace-loving, considerate, submissive, full of mercy
and good fruit, impartial and sincere.*

—JAMES 3:17

One at a time, strangers wearing grim smiles and serious faces filed into the room to join my husband and me at a long, wide table. As I remember it (and I'm sure my memory is exaggerated by the emotions of the experience) the table widened at the end where the professionals sat and became small and tiny on our end, like the view of an airport runway at the opposite end of a landing strip. When the chairs at the table filled up, those remaining sat or stood outside the table, pad and pencils poised, looking terribly bored and important.

I clung to my husband's hand, feeling like a tiny pea under a towering pile of stifling mattresses. As everyone took a chair, the stale air grew thick with tension. Anxiety and fear pressed in, jumbling my thoughts. I caressed the notebooks of information I'd prepared as I tried to calm myself. There was much I wanted to share with these specialists about my boys. I was eager to express my knowledge and ideas, but I was also terrified.

Facing the IEP Dragon

The conference was held to develop the twins' first individualized education plans (IEPs) for kindergarten at the public school. I still felt unsure about our decision to place them in the local elementary school. Since our other children were homeschooled, I assumed the school had prejudged us for choosing that method. I imagined that the preschool had probably shared their "mother from another planet" stories about me with the IEP team.

We'd had a rocky start in Indiana. The services that were abundant for the boys in the state of Arkansas left me ill-prepared for the lack of services in the Hoosier State where we now lived. The rural public school was not as progressive as the developmental center the twins had attended daily in Bentonville. While they had used sign language fluently in Arkansas, they lost most of those skills because the staff in Indiana didn't use sign language. The boys used communication boards in Arkansas, but they weren't provided in Indiana. The instructors didn't seem interested in learning to use them, and as a parent I was apparently not qualified to teach anyone about them. I admittedly grew a bit resentful and felt powerless, since their preschool denied any of my special requests or suggested adaptations for them.

I stared at the shiny name tags pinned to each team member's shoulder, announcing their names and professions: special education teacher, general education teacher, occupational therapist, speech pathologist, physical therapist, school psychologist, school counselor, principal, vice principal, paraprofessional, area program director, case coordinator, school social worker . . . the titles swam before me in a sea of confusion, but they beamed a crystal-clear message in spite of the crashing waves:

WE ARE THE PROS.

You, on the other hand, are just the parents.

The brush-off wasn't intentional. They were doing what they'd always done: squeezed in one more meeting in the midst of an already-overbooked IEP conference season. Organizing such meetings was (and is) a logistical nightmare. Getting each professional to synchronize their schedules with each other was no easy task. And once that occurred, everyone had to come up with a way to be on the same page with the least amount of effort. Time was (and still is) of the essence. To move things along, one had to disarm and pacify overzealous parents in their advocacy for what a young child with autism should receive in an educational setting.

I rubbed my fingertips along my empty shoulder, imagining what my name tag might say if I had one: Exhausted Mom. Determined Mom. You-don't-know-them-like-I-do-or-love-them-like-I-do-or-have-as-many-sleepless-nights-invested-in-them-as-I-do Mom. If the school were to give me one it might have said: Obsessive-helicopter Mom. Must-know-and-understand-her-place Mom. Know-it-all Mom.

Mom-who-must-be-silenced.

Someone spoke. I don't remember who it was or what they said. I heard my heart beating inside my head and felt it pulsate behind my eyes. One by one, each soul in the room introduced themselves. All I could think was how I'd never remember their names, but then how I wouldn't need to because they all wore name tags.

As the meeting progressed, these experts used terms I didn't understand and rattled off enough acronyms to make a cryptologist dizzy. Like a *Peanuts* schoolteacher, their lips moved and sound came out, but mostly what I heard was "wah, wah, wah, wah, wah." I sat and nodded, smiled when I thought it was appropriate, and thought to myself, "I'm never going to get to talk. They keep looking at their watches. They're not interested in anything I have to say."

Even in my state of anxiety and confusion, I was cognizant enough to know that some things didn't make sense. The school practiced full inclusion, which was rather cutting-edge in those days. Full inclusion, also known as mainstreaming—the practice of placing children with disabilities in the general classroom with typical students—wouldn't exactly meet the pressing needs of my boys. I didn't want them to be in a general education classroom and pushed along the daily schedule, simply for the sake of being around typical children. I wanted them to have interventions that could help them overcome the grip autism had on their lives.

I'd read the research. I knew what was working to help children with autism overcome their limitations. The twins couldn't speak, toilet themselves, or modulate their emotions. *Why were we discussing reading and math goals?*

My mind screamed at the illogical conversation taking place. Like a blinding neon banner, it lit up every neuron in my brain.

These people don't get autism. They don't get that what these boys need more than anything is a means to communicate. They don't understand that the primary emotion in autism is fear and that they need sameness. They need to understand that what works well for children with autism—visual cues, schedules, routines—is good for the whole class. They don't get my boys!

I had prepared materials that I wanted included in the IEP and mailed them to the school before the meeting. In hindsight, it was too much. I'd overdone it. Once the meeting concluded, it was clear they had refused to consider any of it. Not once did they acknowledge what I'd sent. My every request was cleverly swept under the rug. But I thought I'd at least try for one little thing.

A smiley face.

Because the twins were nonverbal at the age of five, they couldn't tell me what kind of day they had at school. I longed to communicate with them.

I cleared my throat. "If I provide a notebook, would the teacher be able to send me a smile or frown each day to let me know what kind of day they've had?"

Heads shook and one of the classroom teachers at the far end of the room spoke up: "That's impossible. When we're getting students ready to go home, there just isn't time."

I've learned a lot since that first meeting. I wasn't successful at advocating for my children in those days because I was awkwardly overzealous in sharing information and knew nothing about how to be wise in negotiations. Hopefully you can learn from my mistakes. As I write this, it still bothers me that we, as parents, were basically ignored. I know that every professional in that room was there because they'd earned the right to be there through their training. And most of the professionals I've worked with over the years are excellent at their jobs. But in 2000, the interventional needs of children with autism weren't as well understood by the public schools as they are now. And yet, most public schools in the United States still fail to provide effective educational programs for most of the autism population.

Wisdom and Discernment

Since 2000, I've become a little wiser in my dealing with experts. As I share these tips, I pray you will internalize them as you travel the road of negotiations with educators and other specialists in your child's life.

You Are the Expert on Your Child

God gave your child to you, not to anyone else sitting at a conference table or behind an office desk. Own that fact and never doubt it.

God's Supernatural Wisdom Is Greater Than Human Wisdom

As a Christian, you have an enormous reserve of wisdom to tap into. God assures us in his Word, "If any of you lacks wisdom, you should ask God, who gives generously to all without finding fault, and it will be given to you" (James 1:5). God has never once failed me when I've asked for an answer to a hard question. He has always supplied me with the resources and wisdom to make the best decisions for my children. What he did for me, he'll do for you.

Your Child Is Unique

God created your child to be unique and different from any other child on earth. He knows them best. You can rest in that knowledge and put the burden of how to parent and educate them on his shoulders. The psalmist David wrote: "For you created my inmost being; you knit me together in my mother's womb. I praise you because I am fearfully and wonderfully made; your works are wonderful, I know that full well" (Ps. 139:13–14). If there are any questions about what is best for your child, ask God. He will reveal it to you.

Prayer Works

Pray for clarity, peace, and cooperation before your meetings with professionals. I also pray for favor. There are things we can do in the natural world to help a meeting go well, but never discount the supernatural hand of God in negotiations. Knowing that he goes before you into the fray will give you peace. "The LORD himself goes before you and will be with you; he will never leave you nor forsake you. Do not be afraid; do not be discouraged" (Deut. 31:8).

And if you're feeling frustrated, take time to breathe and remember that God is not surprised by what is going on in the conference. He already knows what's up and how he's going to fix it. "It is not by sword or spear that the LORD saves; for the battle is the LORD's" (1 Sam. 17:47).

God Makes Divine Appointments

Just as God knows you and your child, he knows each person on the committee and has a plan for their life. Our autism walk isn't only about us and our children (shocking, I know). This journey, I believe, is also full of divine appointments. We never know whom we may influence or inspire by our example. You may be thinking, "Are you kidding me? Do you know how overwhelmed I am? I don't have time to worry about being an example!" Believe me, I know. And you're exactly right. Let God do the worrying for you. Let him do the guiding. "In all your ways submit to him, and he will make your paths straight" (Prov. 3:6).

Professionals are people too. They have egos, agendas, schedules, carpooling commitments, soccer games, and families to juggle. Try to truly listen in the meetings and recognize that God has placed these people in your child's life for a reason. Think of the orchestrating of lives he's done to bring you and your child to this moment. How miraculous is our God? From the beginning of time, he knew what your child would need, and he is able to provide it. Recognize the blessing these people are. "He is before all things, and in him all things hold together" (Col. 1:17). Recognize that they are experts too, and respect the years of training and education they've obtained to be where they are now.

Be Bold, Not Pushy

Pray for humble boldness. The battle does belong to the Lord, but he will use us as his instruments to bring his purposes to fruition. There will be times you'll need to be bold in your advocacy for your child. However, there's a difference between spiritual boldness that comes from the Lord and pushiness. We can be assertive and not aggressive. The great thing about being a believer is that we have the confidence that God is fighting with us and for us! We have nothing to fear when we truly understand that God is our child's advocate. I love this word picture in Proverbs 28:1: "The wicked flee though no one pursues, but the righteous are as bold as a lion." People with ulterior motives will run in fear from nothing. But if your motive is purely for the best interest of your child, you have nothing to fear, for "if God is for us, who can be against us?" (Rom. 8:31). You can go forward with boldness.

Listen Well

After a team member tells you what they want you to know, you may consider repeating it back to them so they know you comprehend what they are saying. Validate their feelings by acknowledging them. After all, they are only human. Scripture admonishes us to "be quick to listen, slow to speak and slow to become angry" (James 1:19). Other good Scripture verses about listening:

> The way of fools seems right to them, but the wise listen to advice. (Prov. 12:15)

> To answer before listening—that is folly and shame. (Prov. 18:13)

Season Your Words

Choose your words carefully. Scripture reminds us that "the prudent hold their tongues" (Prov. 10:19) and that "those who guard their mouths and their tongues keep themselves from calamity" (Prov. 21:23). I especially like this verse: "Even fools are thought wise if they keep silent, and discerning if they hold their tongues" (Prov. 17:28). If you listen carefully first, let the other party speak, and acknowledge what they've said, when it's your turn you will find a more receptive audience. In my experience, the less said the better. That doesn't mean you must clam up. I don't mean that at all. What I'm talking about is quality of communication versus quantity. Weigh your words carefully and make them count. "A word fitly spoken is like apples of gold in pictures of silver" (Prov. 25:11 KJV). Sometimes when I'm not sure what to say, I say nothing at all and then write it in an email later if it's something I feel I need to clarify. I also pray silently a lot during meetings, asking the Lord to give me the words to speak, just as he did for Moses when he went before Pharaoh. And, just as Jesus promised the disciples when he sent them forth: "Make up your mind not to worry beforehand how you will defend yourselves. For I will give you words and wisdom that none of your adversaries will be able to resist or contradict" (Luke 21:14–15).

Ask Questions

Ask questions that lead to answers in your child's favor. I wish I'd have understood the power of a question. For example, instead of saying, "My son needs a communication board during snack time," I wish I had asked something like, "How can we help my son communicate his need for a napkin or spoon during snack time?" More than likely the team would have come up with the idea I had in the first place—a placemat communication board. In my experience, educators and therapists are great problem solvers and enjoy solving puzzles. When they themselves invest in the strategy they will more readily use it. This is the sort of wisdom that Jesus used when he taught. As parents we are, in a way, teaching school staff and other professionals about our child. By asking the right questions, we can help them better understand our children and who they are. Jesus used this very strategy with the disciples when he asked them, "Who do the crowds say I am?" and when he asked Peter, "But what about you? . . . Who do you say I am?" and Peter responded, "God's Messiah." (Luke 9:18, 20).

Be a Team Player

Be an ally, not an enemy. Build relationships. If you practice some of the tips I've included in this chapter, you're well on your way to establishing a positive relationship with your child's team. It's important to remember they're human, too, and in need of encouragement. I know that sometimes it feels like "they" don't get "us"—and how can they, unless they've walked in our shoes? They may never extend a compliment or thank you in return, but that's not how Christ has taught us to interact, is it? I find that if I pray for my child's team members, I develop a sense of compassion for them that comes across in my dealings with them. That's not to say I'm a pushover. Jesus wasn't a pushover and he doesn't expect us to be, either. But, he was compassionate and patient with those who didn't get him. As Christians, we're called to walk in a spirit of forgiveness and grace: "Do not judge, and you will not be judged. Do not condemn, and you will not be condemned. Forgive, and you will be forgiven. Give, and it will be given to you. A good measure, pressed down, shaken together and running over, will be poured into your lap. For with the measure you use, it will be measured to you" (Luke 6:37–38).

We may not see results of our graciousness right away, but rest assured that God sees your obedience, and his Word doesn't return void. If you practice this principle, you won't burn bridges. You never know when you may need that individual to help you in the future.

Watch for Fickle Feelings

Don't trust your feelings—trust God. Your emotions will convey false messages. As Christians we walk by faith, not by sight (2 Cor. 5:7). When things seem impossible, they're not. With God all things are possible (Matt. 19:26). Our feelings will deceive us, but God and his word never will.

Have an Attitude of Gratitude

Encourage your child's team members. It's difficult to remember, but if the Lord brings them to your mind during the day, send them a text or email letting them know how much you appreciate them. I know that when I've done this in the past, my note seemed to get to them on the very day they've needed it. Their jobs aren't always easy and they can get discouraged just as we do. I know that for myself, a little encouragement fuels me for days and weeks. I also like to let them know I'm praying for them. Sometimes my sons' staff then share their faith with me and we learn we're siblings in Christ!

During that first IEP conference, I wish I had known what I know now: that God was there with me, holding on to me. And, that he was available to me to guide me through the process. I wish I'd understood that my child's team was just doing their jobs in the same way they'd always done and didn't have time or resources to think outside routine parameters. I also wish I'd have had less of a "me versus them" mentality and more of a "we're all in this together" attitude.

Focusing on my children's strengths and resting in God's perfect plan for my children's lives would have served me much better than wrestling with issues that I should have left in God's hands. Learning how to negotiate would have as well.

Whatever you do, don't let the devil deceive you into thinking you can't do this. Don't let him win by allowing yourself to be tormented with worry and fear. Remember God's words to the children of Israel. What he did for them, he will do for you: "So do not fear, for I am with you; do not be dismayed, for I am your God. I will strengthen you and help you; I will uphold you with my righteous right hand" (Isa. 41:10).

Chapter 6

The Devil Is a Bully but Your Child Has an Advocate

I have forgiven in the sight of Christ for your sake,
in order that Satan might not outwit us. For we are not
unaware of his schemes.
—2 CORINTHIANS 2:10–11

As Christians, we not only have an advocate, Jesus Christ, we also have an enemy. He is called Satan, Lucifer, and the Evil One. There are many other names for him in the Bible. As parents, we must never forget that he truly exists and is the father of lies. He is our greatest foe in life, especially when it comes to raising our children. Every parent knows the most vulnerable place for Satan to strike is at our children. Because he hates us, he'll do all he can to wound us through them. Let me explain why.

Satan hates God, and because he hates God, he hates us—*God's* children—because we are created in our heavenly Father's image. Animals and angels don't have that claim. Because Satan wants desperately to be like God, he's tremendously resentful and jealous of our position with our heavenly Father. He hates us because we worship God when Satan himself desires to be worshipped.

Satan's Worst Nightmare

Satan is tormented by pride and hate. He has a deep loathing for anyone who worships and serves the one true God. He'll do everything he can to throw us off track. I think distraction is one of his favorite schemes, followed by lies. Where your children are concerned, he'll do all he can to discourage you and deceive you. Jesus said that Satan "was a murderer from the beginning, not holding to the truth, for there is no truth in him. When he lies, he speaks his native language, for he is a liar and the father of lies" (John 8:44).

As Christians, Satan has even more reason to discourage and hinder you. When Jesus Christ died and rose again, he reversed the curse of death and separation from God. We have fellowship with God now, just as humans did in the garden of Eden where there was no sickness or disease. That is because there was no sin there. But when Adam and Eve disobeyed God, sin came to the earth and separated God's children from himself because he is holy (Isa. 59:2).

Jesus's death and resurrection bridged the chasm between humans and God. When we accept Christ as our Lord and Savior (simply asking him to come into our hearts and live, confessing we are sinners in need of his forgiveness, and affirming that we believe he is the Son of God), we have the privilege of boldly talking to and fellowshipping directly with God. Not only do Jesus's death and resurrection give us access to God as never before but Jesus also suffered as we suffer. He totally gets it. He knows what it's like to walk this earth, to be yearning souls trapped in frail human bodies:

> Therefore, since we have a great high priest who has ascended into heaven, Jesus the Son of God, let us hold firmly to the faith we profess. For we do not have a high priest who is unable to empathize with our weaknesses, but we have one who has been tempted in every way, just as we are—yet he did not sin. Let us then approach God's throne of grace with confidence, so that we

may receive mercy and find grace to help us in our time of need. (Heb. 4:14–16)

While earth itself is still in its imperfect, fallen state with disease, death, and every form of evil imaginable, our eternal fate is sealed in the shed blood of Christ Jesus. Satan truly hates that as Christ's redeemed children we will live and reign forever with God (2 Tim. 2:11–13). The devil is vengeful and jealous. He hates the finished work of the cross and knows his days are numbered (Rev. 20:1–3, 10). He's out to hurt those God loves most—his beloved children.

Pretending this adversary doesn't exist doesn't mean he's not real and not at work. First Peter 5:8 tells us that our "enemy the devil prowls around like a roaring lion looking for someone to devour." God has a brilliant plan for you, your child, and your family, and Satan is determined to thwart it. The devil wants your child to fail. God wants your child to succeed. And to succeed, your child needs you to walk in truth, not lies.

You Are a Target

As a Christian parent of a child with autism, you are a target for the devil and anyone he chooses to use as a tool. He hates that you are God's hands on this earth, that you have a place in his kingdom, and that you are advancing the Lord's cause. People will have opinions that will hurt you; churches may sometimes be callous due to their ignorance. Recognize that they are not your enemy. Autism isn't even your enemy. Your adversary is a feeble entity that only has the power you give him. James 4:7 says that all you have to do is "resist the devil, and he will flee."

It's okay to be angry about your situation as long as you understand where to direct that anger. Autism didn't exist in the garden of Eden, but when Satan's jealousy caused him to tempt God's children in the garden—and they yielded to the temptation—the earth became imperfect. In its fallen state, humankind's genes, choices, and food sources all became deficient. Our anger should be directed at the destroyer, not the Creator. "For we do not wrestle against flesh and blood, but against principalities, against powers, against the rulers of the darkness of this age, against spiritual hosts of wickedness in the heavenly places" (Eph. 6:12 NKJV).

One of Satan's favorite schemes is to target parents' insecurities and get them to ask questions like: "Is autism my fault? What did I do wrong? Is God punishing me? What if I prayed harder?" or "Maybe I'm not doing enough therapy, going to the right doctors, and feeding them the right food. What if I had given them that vitamin therapy? Not allowed vaccines?" Or say things like: "I shouldn't bother any of my friends by taking my child to the party where he might have a tantrum." And on and on it goes.

As I've written this book, one of the fears the enemy has taunted me with is that the reader will feel condemnation instead of encouragement, peace, and freedom. Don't let that happen, dear reader. There is no condemnation in Christ Jesus (Rom. 8:1). None of us are perfect parents. No one can possibly know the best way to parent a typical child, let alone a child with autism. If this were the case, someone would bottle up the formula and make a fortune!

Don't believe the enemy's lies about your frailties. No one is flawless and everyone is fallible. (If you think you're perfect, perhaps you have an issue with pride!) It's in our weaknesses that God's power is glorified. God hasn't called you to parent this child because you're perfect. He already knows you're not. God has called you because he knows he is able to give you the wisdom and strength to handle it.

While it's okay to have questions for God (it's not like he doesn't know what we're thinking in the first place), it's also important to work at recognizing whether these doubts stem from our own frustrations or the enemy planting false ideas in our heads. It's all in our attitude toward our Lord. Do we have a resentful or a worshipful attitude? Sometimes we may have a bit of both. That's because we're human.

God's truth can handle our doubts because it's perfect.

I'll admit that recognizing when you're being deceived isn't easy. And even good parents will second-guess themselves from time to time. But tormenting yourself with self-doubt will distract you from the next thing you need to do. You can't fix what you did yesterday, but God can. Move on. God isn't going to beat you up about it, so don't beat yourself up.

You Have an Advocate

It's easy to get overwhelmed and feel inadequate. That's when it's time to recognize that you're not going through life with autism by yourself. And frankly, you can't.

That's why you have an advocate. If God is for you, who can be against you? (Rom. 8:31) Think about it. God isn't sitting up on his big throne in heaven pointing a finger at you. He is fighting *for* you.

If you can grasp that the same God who hung the sun the perfect distance from the earth is fighting for you, you will navigate the labyrinth of services and opinions fearlessly. If you have to whisper this to yourself every morning, noon, and night, do it: "The Lord is fighting for me and my child. I need only to be still." One thing autism usually isn't, is peaceful. But knowing we have an advocate can bring us the peace that passes all understanding. By praising God when we're feeling overwhelmed rather than complaining, his presence will get us through the meltdowns, the tiffs with service providers, or the stresses of negotiating with the school. "Rejoice in the Lord always. I will say it again: Rejoice! . . . *Do not be anxious about anything*, but in every situation, by prayer and petition, with thanksgiving, present your requests to God. And the peace of God, which transcends all understanding, will guard your hearts and your minds in Christ Jesus" (Phil. 4:4, 6–7; emphasis mine).

Please understand, I realize that families living with autism experience suffering in different forms. But know this: those without Christ suffer more. This perspective gives us even more reasons to rejoice. We have a blessed hope. In Christ there is always hope. This earthly life is a temporary situation, not a permanent one: "For our light and momentary troubles are achieving for us an eternal glory that far outweighs them all" (2 Cor. 4:17).

Our children with autism are not just bodies and minds. They have spirits too. Their spirits are not autistic. Sometimes I wonder if people with neurological disabilities don't have an even greater sense and understanding of spiritual matters than typical folks. In working with the disability community—specifically people with cognitive impairments, Down syndrome, and autism—I've met some spiritual giants.

My sons, for example, speak with their great advocate, Yahweh, on a constant basis.

"Mama, I prayin' to God last night and he tell me that I gonna do good on my test today at school."

"He did?"

"Yup. An' him also said not worry 'bout it."

How precious is that?

Is it because he advocates for them even more than we do? Is it because special needs children are more capable of approaching God like little children that they hear his voice?

It's something I'm looking forward to visiting with God about in the next life. Oh, I have a lot of questions for him, as I'm sure you do too. But for now, we can rest in his promises:

- He is fighting for us.
- He has a perfect plan.
- He loves our children more than we do.
- He is our advocate.
- "Weeping may endure for a night, but joy comes in the morning" (Ps. 30:5 NKJV).

Even on your weakest days, you and your child with autism are greater than the devil. God's Word tells us that when he lives in us, he is much greater than the enemy and we have his power to overcome anything the devil may try to throw at us (1 John 4:1–4). You and your child are not what the world says you are but what God says you are. Zephaniah 3:17 tells us that God rejoices over us with singing! Imagine the all-powerful God singing and celebrating your life. Wow. What a picture.

God's Word also reminds us that we are raised up with Christ and seated with him in the heavenly realms (Eph. 2:4–6). That makes the devil crazy. He is insanely jealous of our position in Christ Jesus. It's one of the main reasons he hates us so much.

The enemy is also afraid of you; that's why he works so hard to discourage you. He's terrified that you will encourage someone he is trying to discourage. He's mortified at the thought of your rejoicing over serving God in this call of autism. He knows that God is up to something good and there's a miracle waiting for you on the other side, because "the LORD gives strength to his people; the LORD blesses his people with peace" (Ps. 29:11).

When the devil tempted Jesus during our Lord's forty-day fast, Jesus was at his physical weakest. The devil loves to get at us when we're tired and overwhelmed. Why? Because he's that weak. If he had more power, he wouldn't wait until we're in a helpless state. But that's his modus operandi.

Jesus didn't fight back with anything except God's Word. And that's how we can overcome as well. When the enemy whispers to you that God isn't there for you, that you're all alone, and he doesn't care, remember Isaiah 49:14–16: "But Zion said, 'The LORD has forsaken me, the Lord has forgotten me.' 'Can a mother forget the baby at her breast and have no compassion on the child she has borne? Though she may forget, I will not forget you! See, I have engraved you on the palms of my hands; your walls are ever before me.'"

Imagine. You are engraved on the palm of God's hand. What a promise! What a reason to rejoice! Knowing this, can you believe that God has a wonderful plan for you and your family? Knowing this, can you trust that his plan is best? Psalm 32:8 says, "I will instruct you and teach you in the way you should go; I will counsel you with my loving eye on you."

You are God's dream come true. So is your child. So is every person in your family. The Lord gave me this song many years ago; when I'm feeling a little down and alone, I like to make myself sing it:

I made you in the secret place
A place you do not know
And I formed you with my loving hands
And then I let you go
To walk the paths prepared for you
To spread your wings and fly
To choose the road to travel
Whether to live or to die
But don't you know I love you?
You're my dream come true.
I can hardly wait until the day
I see you running in the light of my Son
I can hardly wait until the day
You stand before me and I say, "Well done."
Don't you know—I love you?
You're my dream come true.

Dear reader, you are not alone. You have an advocate.
His name is Jesus.

Chapter 7

Not an Island

Carry each other's burdens, and in this way you will fulfill the law of Christ.
—GALATIANS 6:2

I'm convinced I came marching out of my mother's womb, vigorously waving a flag of independence. (And it's a good thing, too, since she abandoned me at birth, but that's another book.) My stubborn, self-righteous autonomy made asking for help a hard lesson to embrace. The oldest of four children, I'm an overachiever with a stalwart adherence to self-sufficiency, handed down to me by trail-blazing ancestors who fought in the American Revolution and built one of the first schoolhouses in Pennsylvania.

There are few shrinking violets in my DNA. My grandmothers on both sides were saucy, strong, opinionated women. If genetics plays a role in personality development, there was little chance for me to be dependent on anyone for anything.

As a pioneering homeschooling mom, the last thing I ever wanted to do was ask for help. I was quite capable of educating and rearing my children by myself, thank you very much. I didn't need the government, the church, or anyone else to know my business or tell me what to do or how to do it. I charged into motherhood like a proud two-year-old who learns to dress herself while pushing away any offers of help. *Leave me alone. I've got this.*

Enter autism. Autism has a way of grabbing you by the ear and bopping you around like a game of Whac-A-Mole. After two years of little sleep, yelling to be heard above screaming babies, and no friends or family nearby to call on for help, I traded my proud flag of independence for a limp white towel of surrender. I came to the startling reality that I wasn't nearly as self-sufficient as I had imagined. I was utterly worn-out, discouraged, and in need of rescue.

Never Alone

As I've mentioned before, we are never alone. Christ has promised he will always be with us (Matt. 28:20). This is a truth that sustains me each day. But through the years I've learned that God's presence also dwells in physical bodies on this earth. Believe it or not, people who are good at what they do want to help you and your family. I know it's hard to ease up on the reins of control. It's taken me a long time to learn how to delegate. But in the end, I'm glad I did. If I hadn't, I don't think the twins would be where they are today.

This struggle with accepting help reminds me of Peter's attitude when Jesus washed the disciples' feet before the Passover meal. Jesus knew full well that Judas had already decided to betray him. He knew that the disciples would abandon him once he was arrested and that Peter would deny him. And yet, our loving Savior poured water into a basin and tenderly washed the disciples' feet and dried them in humble servitude.

Peter was shocked at this and didn't want Jesus to serve him in this way.

"No," said Peter, "you shall never wash my feet."

Jesus answered, "Unless I wash you, you have no part with me."

"Then, Lord," Simon Peter replied, "not just my feet but my hands and my head as well!" (John 13:8–9)

It takes courage to ask for help because it makes us vulnerable. But like Peter, we miss out on a blessing for ourselves and others if we don't. God's children are called to humility and servitude: "Finally, all of you, be like-minded, be sympathetic, love one another, be compassionate and humble" (1 Peter 3:8). Our pride keeps us from living the abundant life God planned for us. It will also keep others from being blessed by helping us.

Sometimes past experiences cause us to be suspicious of others when we've been disappointed, used, or neglected too many times. Because of our wounds, we promise ourselves to never be vulnerable again. We build walls because of the hurt, thinking we're protecting our hearts, but in reality, we're closing ourselves off from the very things that make life rich and full.

Let's face it, people are busy, and we don't like to impose upon them. The competitive nature of American culture makes us feel that we're inferior if we ask others for help. What if it makes us appear weak or less than perfect? Being judged is a fear we struggle with as well, because people are opinionated and most don't hesitate to share their feelings openly, especially now in this age of social media.

But we have an example in a very personal God who walked this earth as a human being. What if Christ hadn't been willing to take risks? What is more vulnerable than leaving heaven, living on earth, being stripped of all dignity, and dying for our sins on the cross? If all we're asked to do is lay down our own pride for the sake of a better path and a fuller life, why shouldn't we?

Jesus said: "The hour has come for the Son of Man to be glorified. Very truly I tell you, unless a kernel of wheat falls to the ground and dies, it remains only a single seed. But if it dies, it produces many seeds. Anyone who loves their life will lose it, while anyone who hates their life in this world will keep it for eternal life" (John 12:23–25).

Now, I realize this verse has to do with eternal life. But the principle of dying in order to live is the same when applied to dying to our pride and asking for help. If we cling to our pride and our fears, we will miss out on incredible adventures. What's worse, we may be denying our children experiences that God wants them to have. We must reach outside our comfort zone to create the best possible life for our kids.

Aren't you and your children worthy of an outstanding life? Of course you are! Jesus provides us with abundant life, not mediocrity. He knows full well how hard this earth journey is; he lived it. And yet if we're not careful, we can allow our own pride and insecurities to keep us from living the ultimate life available to us.

No one is waiting at the finish line to give you a medal for doing everything yourself. No one will applaud or sing your praises. So why make it more difficult by going it alone?

Surrounding Yourself with Support

Life is hard enough without autism. Life with autism is, at times, overwhelming. Just as I can't imagine living a life without Christ (I honestly don't know how people do it), I also can't imagine living a life without the help that God has provided for me through the years. Were it not for the community of support my husband and I created for the twins, they wouldn't function at the level they do now.

Asking for help doesn't mean throwing up your arms and inviting just anyone to join your team. Obviously, there is the need to protect your family. I believe that if you ask, God will send the right help: "If you, then, though you are evil, know how to give good gifts to your children, how much more will your Father in heaven give good gifts to those who ask him!" (Matt. 7:11).

I'm grateful that God heard and answered my pleas. Through the years, the twins' network of support has grown and changed several times. But whomever God sent, I accepted as the gift that they were, and I'm forever grateful for what they've poured into the twins.

Please understand, my expectations were great. Because I'm fiercely protective of my boys, my standards were high, and I screened those who helped me carefully. Here are some characteristics I felt were most important when choosing helpers.

Sense of Humor Required

Helpers must have a sense of humor. Without a sense of humor, I'd have never survived parenthood, let alone parenting twins with autism. I need helpers who won't be easily overwhelmed and frustrated and can find humor in stressful situations.

When a security guard "stalked" us at a supercenter and then stopped us at the door because he thought (erroneously) that we'd stolen a fountain drink, I needed someone who would laugh with me or keep me calm with humor. Being searched at the exit in front of Walmart shoppers while the twins screamed at the top of their lungs was not only ridiculous but hilarious. My helper at that time was an artistic woman we called Miss Jo. She was funny, energetic, and a little eccentric. When the three-year-old twins drove her van off the side of a small mountain in Bella Vista, Arkansas, she didn't flip out about the damage. (I'll explain this event in more detail later.) When I think of Miss Jo, I think of someone with a huge smile who loved to laugh. She was a perfect fit for us when the twins were preschoolers. And the twins adored her.

At the Mercy of the Judge

Helpers must be nonjudgmental. I need someone who won't criticize the condition of my home or my car or what I feed my kids. I need them to step up beside me and trust my decisions as a mother. I have to admit that in times past I've had to enlist helpers who were critical. However, their attitude toward my home life and decisions was outweighed by the excellent work they did with my children.

Sometimes you do have to tolerate certain flaws to find help. No one is perfect. However, I prefer someone who will keep their judgments to themselves and understand that a home with autism is not going to run like a typical home. We have to let some things go, and sometimes that means a day or two of laundry.

I decided years ago that my children could either have an uptight mom who was a screaming shrew or a mother who was willing to overlook some messes to keep the peace. I chose peace. But in that choice came a lifestyle that other people may not be able to tolerate. I need helpers who will understand our cluttered existence and the reasons behind it. My children are not always tidy. There are holes in the walls, thousands of fingerprints on the windows, and broken furniture from autism meltdowns. Sometimes the dishes and laundry are neglected because of the interruptions of the constant supervision my boys require. At times, I'm too mentally, emotionally, and physically exhausted to do anything but stare off into space once they are asleep. Other days I'm simply overwhelmed and don't know where to start. My attitude is that if someone is critical of our life and the condition of my home or yard, they can lend a helping hand to make it better. Amazingly, I've yet to find a line of people at my door eager to volunteer.

A Little Privacy, Please

Helpers must practice confidentiality. Anyone who works with my children must agree to keep my family business, and my twins' activities with them, in the strictest confidence. This is nonnegotiable. When I learned that a worker was driving around with my child's medical records in her car, I let her go. I do not allow helpers to post anything about their activities with my twins on the Internet without my permission. Their privacy must be protected—period.

R-E-S-P-E-C-T

Helpers must be respectful. I need someone who will honor the sanctity of my home. But more importantly, they must respect my children as individuals, with all the rights and privileges that anyone else would enjoy. I also need someone to respect me as the mom, my husband as the dad, and my other children as part of the family home.

They also need to be tactful. Through the years, as a pastor's wife and a mother, I've worked with various people who failed to filter their opinions before speaking. Being tactful and weighing one's words carefully is something I look for in a helper. The frustration level can be high when working with my children, and I need someone who can bite their tongue and not say everything they're thinking, especially when we're out in public. Cursing, of course, is absolutely unacceptable, since one of the traits of autism is to parrot words back. I didn't need young sons using bad words they couldn't understand.

Double-Jointed Flexibility

Helpers must be flexible. If you've lived with autism for very long, you're likely as malleable as a double-jointed circus contortionist. When I was being trained as a court-appointed special advocate, I was asked whether or not I was flexible. My answer? "I have twins with autism. Is that flexible enough for you?" I know for myself, at least, it's hard to be spontaneous or hope for a plan to come together perfectly. I used to be extremely organized and an avid pre-planner. And while I do believe structure is vitally important, I've had to accept that not all things will go according to my design. It makes submitting to God's ideas for the day an absolute necessity. What a gift we have in this lesson! "Many are the plans in a person's heart, but it is the LORD's purpose that prevails" (Prov. 19:21). Our helpers must be flexible and willing to bend their wills, minds, and emotions to the needs and demands of my children.

Nobody Knows Everything

Helpers must be teachable. This is a tough one because, in my experience, hard-working, responsible people tend to be strong self-starters and sometimes set in their own ways. But I need my helpers to take my advice and direction willingly. I also need to lead well and help the worker take ownership of my ideas. As I mentioned in chapter 5, asking the right questions helps people arrive at favorable conclusions.

Stressed Is Desserts Spelled Backward

Helpers must be able to handle stress maturely and appropriately. There are tremendous pressures in working with the children, meeting deadlines, doing paperwork, and interacting with me, the parent. If a helper is easily upset, defensive, or frustrated, this isn't the job for them.

Outside-the-Box Thinkers

Helpers must be creative. Besides her wonderful laid-back personality and sense of humor, Miss Jo's greatest skill was coming up with ideas for preventing meltdowns. She was the one who taught me, the mom, to have the twins wave bye-bye to McDonald's when we drove past so they wouldn't throw a tantrum. When we lived in the Bentonville/Rogers area of Arkansas, there was more than one McDonald's to pass on our way to anywhere. Fries were their favorite food when they were three, and whenever we passed they would cry and use sign language and scream, "Fies! Fies!" (In fact, they said "fies" before they ever said "Mama" or "Daddy"!)

Miss Dianna was extremely skilled at keeping the twins on a schedule and providing daily structures and routines (something I'm not as good at). Miss Mary's greatest skill was her bottomless barrel of patience and her ability to "go with the flow." Their helper, Miss Ruth, was excellent at keeping them meaningfully engaged and looking for ways to motivate and redirect them. Every assistant brought a different type of skill to the table, and I tried to keep those talents in mind on the days I second-guessed my decision to ask for help.

Background Checks

Helpers must have pristine background checks. I've been shocked through the years at the rise in convictions of violent child abusers and sex offenders. I highly recommend every worker in your home have a background check. If you hire through an agency they usually perform these before sending someone to work with you. However, do your own investigating. Check their online social media activity and do a Google search of their name. I'm amazed at how much information people willingly share on the Internet.

Love and Boundaries

Helpers must be firm but loving. The twins needed (and still need) someone who would stand their ground on important battles. Miss Dianna (whom I called their "other mother" when they were growing up) was structured and firm. She was much firmer than I was and managed to win nearly every battle the twins dragged her into. They needed this tenacious discipline growing up, and I credit her with a lot of the twins' success as adults today. What a godsend this woman was! Her determination and work ethic served the twins very well. I consider her influence in their life a true miracle. And I often wonder: What if I had given in to my insecurities and not asked her for help? I hate to think where we might be.

Our helpers through the years weren't always what I call "hired friends." When the twins were babies, we had a revolving door of teen boys who hung around to visit with our beautiful teenage daughter. If there were free hands and arms, I recruited them. If visitors stayed for dinner, they were enlisted as stroller-pushers while I cooked the meal. In those days, there was no consoling the twins. They screamed nonstop no matter how vigorously the teens walked them, but it freed my hands, and the teens didn't care what they were doing as long as they were hanging out at our place.

Avoiding Isolation

It's far too easy to isolate ourselves because we're afraid of being hurt. Distrust is a powerful tool the enemy uses to deceive us. In fact, he used it in the garden of Eden when he convinced Adam and Eve that they couldn't trust God to tell them the truth. It caused them to question the very One who created them in his image with his loving hands. It's easy to fall into the trap of distrust and fear, but with God's help we can conquer this tendency and create a richer life for our children and ourselves.

My experience in recruiting help hasn't always gone well, and I admit there have been times when working with some of them that I've experienced hurt, disgust, and disappointment. But I can say with full confidence that sticking my neck out and asking for support has brought my family many more blessings than burdens.

God will use all sorts of unusual ways to send you help if you let him. Never underestimate how clever he is. God is faithful. When we ask for help, he sends it. I can't think of one instance when I asked for help that he didn't give it to me.

God doesn't prefer me over you.

If you ask him, he will send help to you too.

Chapter 8

Make the Screaming Stop

As a mother comforts her child, so will I comfort you.
—ISAIAH 66:13

Every morning before the twins opened their eyes, they screamed. High-pitched, ear-piercing, and nonstop wails. Sometimes, in the pink light of dawn, I cried too. How could I face another day of being unable to console my children? Something was wrong. But no one would listen to me.

This wasn't the normal fussiness of a child crying because they were wet or hungry or sleepy. This was full-out, earsplitting shrieking, as if they were being beaten or in intense pain. Feeding them was difficult since they would scream in the midst of drinking their bottles. Bathing didn't go well either, because they were terrified of water on their skin. (They still don't like it.) Dressing them exhausted me. They fought my efforts and cried so hard that sometimes I feared they'd have a seizure, with their bodies stiffened and their faces burning purple-red with rage. It was a bit frightening and definitely nerve-racking.

Another troubling behavior started after they learned to crawl. Every day they'd bite each other on the back—hard enough to draw blood. I didn't learn until later that this was typical of twins, but their biting was different. They'd munch down and not let go. Rescuing the victim was like trying to extract a juicy bone from a pit bull.

Nothing I did pleased them. There were no smiles, no babbling, and no reciprocation of affection. It was in those first years that I came to understand how parents snap. I'm thankful for the grace that got me through those hardest moments. Unless you live in the pressure cooker of the relentless chaos of autism, you can't know.

Mealtime was an exhausting battle, too. We finally learned they did better in the dining room alone, away from the family, while we ate in the kitchen. I placed their high chairs on two large plastic tablecloths on the floor. A window cutout between the dining room and kitchen allowed me to keep an eye on them. As long as others weren't around, they ate peacefully. But if the other children drew near, they went into meltdown mode. Food ended up everywhere but in their mouths. My kitchen walls looked like a modern art exhibit.

It breaks my heart when I read of children with disabilities being murdered or abused by their parents. However, while I abhor it, I understand how it happens. Parents burn out because of a lack of support. When I read the news reports it makes me wish someone—anyone—could have come along beside the parent and helped carry their load. If you're reading this book and you don't have a child with autism, offer help to those who do. Then provide it. You may just save a family or life.

Sensory Processing Disorder

I knew in my heart that the twins' nervous systems were out of whack. They couldn't console themselves, and nothing comforted them. They were miserable, tiny creatures with the robust lungs of Metropolitan Opera singers. The only time they were completely quiet was when they went to sleep, and even then they slept fitfully. I wasn't able to rock them to sleep or cuddle them because they arched their backs and fought me. But usually I bundled them tightly and held them anyway. Instinctively I knew they needed that. They'd wear themselves out screaming, sleep for a few hours, and wake up crying again.

Sometimes, during the day, we put them in baby swings. That worked for a few minutes, but not always. There was only one thing that gave us more than a few minutes of peace, and I looked forward to those minutes all day, every day.

In the evenings after dinner, we bundled them in their car seats and buckled them in the back seat of my daughter's car. It was an old, banged-up Chrysler LeBaron in need of a new muffler. You could hear that car from blocks away, but the loud noise and movement calmed the twins every evening for about thirty minutes. Sometimes they'd even fall asleep.

But as soon as they were out of that car, the screaming commenced. Walking them in strollers didn't work, singing to them didn't work, and no amount of jiggling or interacting with them calmed them in those early days.

I searched the Internet for clues. I discovered that their constant screaming could be a symptom of a newly discovered, controversial syndrome now called sensory processing disorder (SPD). The twins exhibited all the following symptoms that are a part of SPD:[1]

- Crying and arching back while being held
- Distressed by diaper/clothing changes
- Upset by bathing or water splashing
- No predictable sleep/wake cycle
- Excessive crying (more than a half hour or hour at a time)
- Doesn't smile
- Can't calm no matter what you try except for one thing, such as a car ride
- Tantrums many times a day
- Troubled by sunlight or bright lights
- Anxious in public places, especially if crowded or noisy
- Doesn't enjoy interactive games such as peekaboo
- Doesn't play with new toys or notice them
- Uses only one hand (can't switch hand to hand)

- Can't clap hands
- Late learning to talk, walk, gesture, hold bottle, and sleep through the night
- Can't use utensils well for age
- Frequent head banging, hitting, biting, pinching, or hurting self or others

Because the twins were first placed in our home as foster children before our adoption was final, we were plugged into home intervention services from the beginning. Through their occupational therapist, I learned more about SPD. She taught me the fine art of infant massage. At first, I thought it was nothing more than a glorified way of slathering on baby lotion. But the more I read about how infant massage helped to calm babies, the more enthusiastic I became.

Over time, I learned that the twins needed firm touch and deep pressure to feel better. As they grew, they ripped the sheets off their mattresses nightly and crawled underneath the mattresses to sleep. They continued to do this well into their teens. Even now, when they are upset, the only way I can help them to calm is to vigorously rub their arms and backs or squeeze their elbow joints. All of this is part of what their systems crave.

I accidentally discovered their need for sensory stimulation. Their older brothers had received a toy called a Bumble Ball Bolter for Christmas. This comical toy had six long legs, with tennis shoe-shaped feet attached to a ball that vibrated, causing the toy to jump up and down. Attached to the top of the ball was a head, with Ping-Pong ball–like eyes and a thatch of fuzzy hair on a long spring. When you turned the toy on, it jumped in place. It was a lot of fun to watch and made us laugh.

The feet of the Bumble Ball Bolter were rubbery. One day I walked into the living room to find the twins sucking on them while the toy was bouncing. They appeared to love the vibration of the toy, as well as the rubbery texture of the feet. It kept them quiet for the few seconds they were able to latch on to it. Unfortunately, due to their developmental delays, they weren't able to hold on to the toy, but they searched for its feet with their mouths. This was another clue that the twins craved a "sensory diet." (See appendix E for more information on SPD.)

One of the reasons children on the autism and fetal alcohol spectra cry and throw tantrums frequently is because of their nervous systems not receiving proper messages. Their senses don't organize into appropriate responses. That's why the twins threw their sippy cups at me even though they were thirsty and why the feeling of water on their skin was (and is) painful. Sensory signals get caught up in sort of a traffic jam. This prevents appropriate information from reaching the brain so that it can interpret sensory data correctly. Anxiety is a huge piece of the sensory puzzle; I believe it is the main reason the twins were miserable, even as infants. In short, they were terrified. Of everything.

At the age of eighteen months, the twins learned to walk. It was during this time that I finally realized their primary emotion was fear. They were afraid of every situation and met every transition from one activity to another with a tantrum. They screamed getting out of bed; they howled going into bed. They bawled going into their high chairs and shrieked coming out. When thirsty, they cried for a sippy cup but promptly threw it at me and wailed when I handed it to them. Day-to-day activities were exhausting and exasperating. Nothing made sense in their world. As frustrated as I was with them at times, my empathetic heart broke for them. *What is it like to be trapped in such a terrifying world? What must it be like to be miserable and frightened all the time?*

Looking back, I honestly don't know how our family held it together. During this period I learned to tolerate and even be thankful for some of the twins' favorite, endlessly repetitive behaviors. As long as they weren't screaming, I didn't care that they were opening and closing doors a thousand times, or flipping the lights on and off. If they weren't screaming, I was thrilled to let them occupy themselves emptying linen drawers and kitchen cabinets. (Later I'd learn this wasn't a good thing to encourage, but thankfully God did teach me along the way.)

Like autism, SPD is different in everyone. For example, some people are more tolerant of tags in their shirts than others. Some people, like me, don't like to wear shoes. (If I'm home, I'm barefoot.) These are sensory preferences. But people with SPD have extreme partialities. For some, the mere feeling of clothing next to their skin is painful. For others, textures of certain foods bother them. When I was small, I remember hating peas because they were squishy. I also refused to wear certain clothes because of the way they felt on my skin. I may have a few SPD issues myself, but nothing like what my twins experience.

In the same way that some sensations are over-exaggerated, they can also be under-interpreted. Children with this disorder may not respond appropriately to pain or temperature. In the middle of tantrums, the twins would bang their heads on concrete sidewalks and show no response to how painful it must have been. Some children are misdiagnosed as having ADHD or labeled as thrill seekers because they crave constant movement or have no fear of dangerous play activities, such as jumping from a high piece of playground equipment.

More Awareness Today

Thankfully, schools and teachers are more aware of this disorder than they were when the twins were small. Now, informed educators are more willing to provide modifications for such children, such as sensory toys and gel seats. I feel blessed that the Lord led us to Arkansas and to Sunshine School, where cutting-edge therapies were available during their preschool years. It was through Sunshine School that I learned important tools for helping the twins with their anxiety. Here's what worked for us then.

Weighted Vests and Blankets

The theory behind the use of weighted vests and blankets to help calm children with autism or SPD is that their bodies crave proprioceptive (meaning sensory) input. The twins craved the sensation of deep pressure—that's why they slept under their mattresses. Proprioception is thought of as a sixth sense of the nervous system; it's what keeps track of the different parts of the body. A child whose brain doesn't process these messages may feel as if they are floating in space. Imagine the anxiety that creates.

When the twins were small, weighted vests only came in a loose-fitting fashion. Now there are vests with tighter compression; I wish they had been available in those days. Such items are expensive, but I know mothers who have created weighted blankets and vests with removable cloth packets of beans or rice (for the weights) for a fraction of the cost. For the twins, wearing the vests helped them to calm down during quiet activities, such as sitting still for a short few minutes in church.

So Many Books, So Little Time!

When the twins were small, I read every book I could get my hands on about autism. In those days there weren't nearly as many as there are now. My favorites included *Thinking in Pictures* by Temple Grandin and *The Out-of-Sync Child* by Carol Kranowitz. I can't emphasize enough what a difference a good book on autism can make for a frazzled mom. Just knowing other people existed who understood what I was going through brought great comfort. And the things I learned from those books helped me feel a little more equipped to face another challenging day of bathtub and bedtime wars.

Transition Toys

The twins fought every transition, especially when going into the church building from the van, and vice versa. My husband is a minister, so we had no choice but to attend church. I'm grateful for this requirement because otherwise I think I'd have given up and stayed home. I credit the twins' saturation in public places, such as church, with their ability to handle public places today.

When they were about two to three years old, they were fascinated with emergency vehicles. I bought a toy police car for each of them and used it as a "transition object" to get them into the van, out of the van, and into their Sunday school room. They couldn't hold the car until they got into the van. Then once we arrived, to hold the toy again, they had to get out of the van. To encourage them to go into the church building, we talked to them about showing their special cars to their Sunday school teacher. When they got to her class, she had another emergency vehicle toy to show them to get them into the room. We tried to arrive early, before the other students, to allow them some time to spend in a transition room before they went in the regular classroom. (I write more about church attendance in chapter 18.)

Viewing the World Through Their Eyes

I learned everything I could about autism so that I could understand its "culture." I wanted to know what motivated my sons' odd behaviors. I desperately needed to connect; I yearned to enter their world and let them know I was in it with them. I knew from reading books and chatting with people online that my boys lived in a world of unrelated experiences and demands. Very little made sense to them. They weren't able to make the connection between getting in the van and going somewhere fun.

I learned about the meaning of the words "hidden curriculum." For example, when typical people get on an elevator, they know there is a hidden curriculum—a kind of societal rule—of facing the door and keeping our hands to ourselves. My sons with autism can't know or pick up on this socially appropriate behavior. That's something they have to be taught. Understanding this, I was better able to prepare them for social situations and avoid meltdowns. I was also able to explain things better to people when the twins greeted them by slapping them—that was how they said hello. (Yes, this really happened on a regular basis to adults in our church. Believe it or not, a slap was a compliment from these guys.)

Schedule Cards and Social Stories

I'm so thankful God invented the computer in time for me to use it for writing social stories. I'm not an artist; I can barely draw a stick figure. I found pictures on the Internet of situations that I wanted to help the twins to understand and glued them onto index cards to create stories to prepare them for new situations. They needed predictability. Keeping the same schedule at home every day helped when the twins were small, but being a pastor's family, that wasn't always possible for us.

Saturation Technique

I'm thankful that our lifestyle failed to limit them. I'm grateful they were forced to be in situations that I'd otherwise have kept them from. I call this my "saturation technique," and it served them very well. My theory is that by exposing them on a regular basis to social situations they were initially scared of, they actually became desensitized to them. We didn't do this without support. I didn't put them in sink-or-swim situations or set them up to fail. They always had the emotional support of a caring adult. But they participate in a lot of things typical children whose parents aren't in ministry wouldn't have to.

For most families, it's too easy to avoid social activities. Quite frankly, it's so much work, both physically and emotionally. People stare and they don't understand. They are critical and point, or criticize and whisper. But because we had no choice but to bring the twins with us to our "job" at the church, they were exposed to much more than they would have been otherwise.

Having to deal with new situations more than the average child with autism served the boys well in the end. They are extremely socially appropriate today and able to handle complex social situations, such as weddings and funerals. When I heard them tell their special education teacher they were "sorry for her loss" on the phone when a loved one passed away, I was extremely proud of them. Because of being preacher's kids, they've learned how to comfort people in difficult situations.

Medications

The twins still struggle to modulate their emotions, but it's much easier to help them understand. After their diagnoses, with the guidance of several doctors, we agreed to try psychotropic medications to help them. We've been blessed because we found the right ones early in the process. Some parents have to go through dozens and never find anything that works. I also realize that other parents choose not to use such medicines, and I don't fault them for it. My journey is not their journey. My children are my responsibility and I'm not sorry we chose to use what science has provided. Once we found the correct prescriptions for the twins, life didn't magically become perfect, but it was more manageable.

My argument for using such treatments is this: with medication, my boys' nervous systems are able to modulate to a level that allows them to be the best they can be. They were able to learn to speak and were much less terrified of the world around them. It didn't change or sedate their personalities. Instead, it allowed them to shine through. We've been fortunate because we haven't had the horrible side effects that some people experience. In this I realize we are extremely blessed. I never take it for granted. Ever. I'm constantly thankful for the science that has allowed the twins to live free from some of the terrors of life.

It's not a cure by any means, but with the help of the medication they have the chance to calm down enough to learn. We can now eat meals as a family and sit around the Christmas tree and open gifts together— things we couldn't do before. God has certainly blessed us in this area of our journey. And I learned a lot about my Lord during the years of their screaming and crying.

Just as I was attentive to the cries of my babies, God is attentive to my cry. I never doubt that now. God knows when something is wrong, and he longs to help us the way I longed to help my boys. His love for us is unconditional, and he doesn't judge us for our frailties. He just wants to comfort us. I know this full well.

"The righteous cry out, and the LORD hears them; he delivers them from all their troubles" (Ps. 34:17).

Chapter 9

Communicating and Connecting

Set a guard over my mouth, LORD; keep watch over the door of my lips.
—PSALM 141:3

At the end of their first year of attending Sunshine School, the twins were three years old. It was no secret that my favorite people at that school were the speech pathologists. Each twin had his own therapist, which thrilled me. So often identical twins are lumped together and seen as one entity instead of separate individuals.

At the end of the year, the school gave an informal awards ceremony. When Isaac got an award for making the "b" sound, my husband and I were as proud as if he'd received a gold medal at the Olympics. We knew how hard he'd worked to make that sound. I can still remember the feeling of pure joy in my chest. I wanted to strut like a peacock, shake the certificate in the air, and shout, "Look what my little boy did!"

What I truly appreciated about the speech therapists at Sunshine School was that they gave me tangible tools to work with. Whatever they used at school, I was given to use at home. I enthusiastically embraced the picture exchange program they introduced as well as their sign-language method (Signing Exact English).

I'm a firm believer in the idea that behavior is communication, especially in nonverbal children. The hard part for parents of children with autism, especially in the teen years, is identifying whether behavior stems from autism, a simple attitude of disobedience, or a comorbid (the presence of more than one disease) condition, such as oppositional defiant disorder. But in my experience with little ones, many meltdowns are a result of frustration at not being able to talk. Once children develop a way to communicate, the anxiety and frustration they experience is lessened exponentially.

Speech and Language

For children with a form of autism called Asperger's syndrome, language may come impressively early; such children appear to have advanced skills (although many children with Asperger's have delayed speech.) They impress their parents and those around them with their amazing memories and their ability to rattle off random facts with alarming accuracy. A friend's teenage son with Asperger's can mimic all his favorite comics and retell jokes he's heard with excellent timing. But when he calls to ask if my boys can come spend the night, he struggles to put together a coherent sentence. The give-and-take of a conversation is difficult for him.

This reveals the difference between the acquisition of language and speech. Speech includes articulation of sounds and putting them together to make words. When a person has difficulty producing sounds correctly, this is a speech disorder. When someone struggles with expressive language, understanding what someone says, or how to put a sentence together fluently, that's a language disorder.

My friend's son has a language disorder only. His articulation is impeccable. But the twins have both a speech and language disorder. They struggle to this day to be understood due to apraxia of speech. In other words, they understand what people say, but their brains don't coordinate their muscles in a way that allows them to make words.

In regards to language, the twins put words in the wrong order. However, they are continuing to improve. One of the great things about texting and social media is that it gives them a lot of practice writing sentences. It's adorable, though, that they write the same way they talk. Even though their language isn't perfect, it's part of their charm. And now these young fellows who struggled to put a sentence together at the age of nine are hard to keep quiet. Their favorite items these days are their cell phones; they are constantly calling people or texting. That's typical teen behavior some parents bemoan, but I rejoice over it!

However, when they were two to three years old, they couldn't speak, and gesturing or pointing was difficult. They didn't wave bye-bye or show others their toys. I tried to engage them with dolls or stuffed animals, but they showed no interest. Before Sunshine School, I was unsuccessful in teaching them how to communicate.

I remember one incident very clearly when Isaac was almost two. He was sitting on the staircase of our home when he said, "Baby." I celebrated and asked him to repeat the word, but he withdrew and never said the word again until the age of seven. I often wonder to this day what allowed his brain to say that word. And what went to work to immediately to shut it off? What a marvelous mystery our brains are!

In my experience, communication and social skills are the two most important abilities to focus on in the early years. Unfortunately, the public school system isn't set up this way. Instead, its focus is more on academic goals because schools are educational institutions. In the United States there is a huge disconnect in treating the child in a holistic manner. This is why I believe Sunshine School was such a success. They integrated all therapies into the classroom. They rarely compartmentalized them. I'll discuss more about this in my chapter on education.

Communication Cards, Pictures, and Schedules

Before the twins got their diagnoses, I realized they were speech delayed. Thankfully, as I've mentioned, God gave them two incredible speech therapists at Sunshine School who taught me how to communicate with the boys. We used sign language (the Signing Exact English method) but we also used a lot of pictures. I used pictures to help them understand what we would do next, and I encouraged them to use pictures to communicate their needs to me. They wore a little pad of photographs on a key ring attached to their belt loop. (We used photographs before transitioning to line drawings. For very young or severely delayed children, line drawings may be too abstract.) My favorite picture tool was a place mat we used at meal time. Meal times provide an excellent opportunity to work on picture communication because the child is eager to communicate they want "more" or a "spoon" or a "drink." The place mat had pictures of these items. You can see a photo of one I made on my website (KarlaAkins.com).

I taught them sign language for many nouns. Of course, with limited fine motor skills (the ability to coordinate hand and finger movements), they modified their signs by inventing their own signs for some objects and for each other. It was an exciting time teaching them "cup," "drink," "more," and "cookie." I still smile remembering how they signed for "cookie" and made the "k" sound twice, "K-K," while their little hands pounded together for one of their favorite snacks.

Waiting was extremely difficult for them, but I taught them the hand signs for "wait," "stop," and "no." It didn't always work, but it helped them understand what Mama wanted. I also printed eight-by-ten pictures for everything I thought they'd need to communicate and hung them in every room of the house. I made a stop sign for them to touch when I wanted them to discontinue a behavior, then would take them to the picture and have them touch it. Of course, putting my hand over theirs was something they didn't tolerate much at first. Eventually, with persistence, they tolerated my guidance more and more.

I also knew I had to help them understand that hitting and biting were off-limits. By the age of four, they rarely pummeled me on purpose. (Admittedly, they do still get physical with one another at times; we're still working on it.) I used short corrections and very few words: "No hit" or "No bite." Children with autism don't hear long explanations. Words get jumbled in their minds if you lecture them.

With consistent correction, their dad and I taught them that hitting, kicking, pulling hair, and biting were definite no-nos. "Use your words," I'd say. They knew that meant "use your pictures" or "use your sign language" or "point to what you need."

Another thing I'm thankful for is that my husband never treated them as if they weren't capable. Neither did any of their helpers. One thing parents should remember is that while a child with autism may not be able to communicate what they know, it doesn't mean they are ignorant. They know much more than most people give them credit for. I knew early on that the twins' receptive language was much more advanced than their expressive language. They understood quite well what we said.

Behavior Is Communication

When looking for reasons behind a child's behaviors, it's important to remember that when they misbehave it's usually for two reasons:

1. To get stuff
2. To avoid stuff

Children with autism often don't have the language skills to get their needs met. So for them, behavior *is* communication. For example, when the twins were smaller, they hated getting ready for bed and would throw themselves on the floor and scream. By doing this, they avoided getting into their pajamas. Or, if they were playing with a toy and threw a fit when asked to share, I wouldn't press the issue because I wanted to avoid a meltdown. As a result, they got more time to play with the toy.

Often, behavior is about both getting *and* avoiding stuff. This is why children escape and run. If I tell the twins to come inside and do their chores and they jump into the pool, they get to swim and avoid doing their chores. Their behavior says, "I want to swim and I don't want to do chores."

Sometimes as parents we don't address behavior for selfish reasons. We want to avoid the confrontation or simply crave another five minutes of peace. But when we do this, we delay our children's development. I'm not saying you don't need to pick your battles. You need to weigh the importance of each incident. But for major issues, ignoring and enabling bad behavior can also damage family relationships. Siblings grow resentful and marriages get stressed. Time is robbed from other family members because when problem behaviors are tolerated, chaos prevails.

Consistency and diligence were (and are) keys when dealing with behavior. My own education also helped. Thankfully, I'm a voracious reader. And as any parent knows, we will read anything we can get our hands on to help our child. (My booklist is in appendix E.) I am grateful to authors, such as Temple Grandin and Stephen Shore, who taught me so much in those early days.

Learning and Setting Goals

I studied what a child with autism must learn to acquire the skills to socialize and communicate. I instinctively knew (I believe the Holy Spirit taught me) that if my children couldn't communicate and socialize, it would impede their progress as functioning adults. It doesn't matter how smart they are or whether or not they can do algebra. If children can't function in a socially appropriate way, it will be difficult for them to keep a job, maintain friendships, and live a full and happy life as an adult.

I made a checklist of milestones I wanted the boys to reach, compiling the list from different resources in print and on the Internet. I also asked for input from Sunshine School's therapists. In the beginning, between the ages of two and three, the list looked something like this:

- Able to sit in a chair alone, one minute per year of age
- Able to sit and play turn-taking game with adult, up to five minutes
- Respond to name
- Respond to "no," "stop," and "wait"
- Sign "wait" back to adult when told to wait
- Imitate up to ten signs for nouns, such as "cookie," "toy," "bus," "cup," "fries," "drink," "bed," "bath," "dog," and "cat."

- Imitate up to ten signs for verbs/adverbs, such as "wait," "go," "bye," and "more."
- Imitate up to ten signs for people, such as "Mama," "Daddy," and names of siblings and familiar people
- Imitate movement to music
- Imitate during playtime
- Imitate using a crayon
- Imitate using a spoon
- Greet familiar people with "hello"
- Point to body parts when asked to "touch your _____"
- Follow one-step instruction such as "pick up your toy"
- Point to pictures in a book
- Imitate sounds
- Point to picture or use sign language instead of crying or grunting to get needs met
- Answer "yes" or "no" with head gesture, sign, or picture

These were the basic skills I knew the twins needed to learn before we could ever show them how to dress themselves, toilet train, or begin pre-academic skills. At this point their main activities when not engaged by another person were emptying toy bins and screaming. Interacting one-on-one with another person for several hours each day was the only way they could make progress. I was grateful they were engaged at Sunshine School during the day. And when they were home, my husband, the other children, my helpers, and I continued the engagement as intensely as we could.

Each one of these milestones had to be broken down into tiny steps, such as those used in Applied Behavioral Analysis (ABA) therapy. For example, for the twins to learn to ask for a cookie instead of crying, it took days of work to teach them to point to a picture of a cookie or sign for it. To teach pointing, I placed my hand over theirs and helped them point to the cookie and immediately gave them a bit of it. Eventually, when I could tell they were catching on, I stopped placing my hand over theirs. They are clever boys and learned that pointing to a picture was a faster way of getting what they wanted.

I used tiny crackers, cereal bits, or other preferred objects to teach them because I learned the best way to reach them was through their favorites. Whatever their obsession, I used it to motivate them to learn. I continued this practice through the years when I homeschooled them; I still use it. I believe this is the best way to teach and motivate any child, but especially children with neurological or cognitive disabilities.

What About Professional Therapy?

Scientists agree that the earlier in life a child receives treatment and therapy, the better their prognosis. Some children improve more than others, but the science shows that as soon as children are diagnosed, they should participate in programs that focus on developing communication, social, and cognitive skills.

The therapies available now that are proven most effective include ABA, occupational therapy, speech therapy, physical therapy, and pharmacological therapy. The purpose of treatment isn't to cure autism but to maximize the quality of life for the child by minimizing the deficits and features of autism.

Applied Behavioral Analysis

ABA helps the child by encouraging positive behaviors and discouraging negative ones. It brings the child to the place where they are able to learn new skills and how to generalize them to new situations. Other forms of ABA are early intensive behavioral intervention (EIBI), used with children younger than five years old, and pivotal response training, which focuses on language, play, and social skills. The most common form of ABA is discrete trial teaching. Each skill is broken down into small steps; prompts and rewards are used in the beginning but phased out as the child grasps the concept. Two other methods that use ABA are the Lovaas Model and the Early Start Denver Model.

Beware of those ABA programs that use extreme aversive reinforcement.

Personally, I believe that positive reinforcement is the only type of reinforcement needed in therapy situations. I'm suspicious of any therapist or teacher who would be harsh with a child in my presence. If they are this way when I'm in the room, how will they be when I'm gone?

ABA is very expensive if your insurance doesn't cover it. It wasn't a well-known, proven therapy when my twins were small. It is much more recognized now, and I'm happy that some insurances now pay for it.

We couldn't afford ABA therapy nor could we pay someone to come into our home and perform any of the other expensive therapies out there. But I could get on the floor and interact with the boys and imitate them, like those who subscribe to Dr. Stanley Greenspan's Floortime Approach therapy. I learned how to use reinforcers and implement them in our day-to-day activities, and I posted pictures all over the house and taught them to touch them to communicate what they wanted.

Speech Therapy

Speech therapy is another proven therapy that's a necessary piece of an autism treatment plan. It's best to use an integrated approach so that parents, teachers, families, and peers are able to communicate in the same way in different situations. As previously mentioned, for nonverbal children, sign language and picture communication programs are important tools when helping to improve communication skills. Once communication is facilitated, many negative behaviors cease.

Occupational Therapy

Occupational therapy is used to help with sensory integration disorders as well as to improve fine motor skills. It can include helping a child learn to dress, use utensils, cut with scissors, and use a crayon or pencil. Each program is individualized, based on the areas the child needs help with most. If a child has severe deficits in sensory motor skills, therapy may include a sensory experience and a sensory diet checklist for parents to use at home. The list may include play activities that are designed to change how the brain responds to touch, sound, sight, and movement.

Physical Therapy

Physical therapy is used to improve gross motor skills and to help a child be more aware of their body in space. The therapist will design a program that helps teach and improve balance, coordination, walking, and sitting. Some physical therapists will use hippotherapy—therapeutic horseback riding—as part of the program. (Occupational therapists may use this as well.) While there are no autism studies regarding the use of hippotherapy, there are empirical studies for using this therapy with children with cerebral palsy and spinal cord injuries. (See appendix E for more information.)

Therapy Techniques at Home

If you're like me and you don't have the funds to pay for an intensive program like ABA, or you live in a rural area as I do and it takes an exorbitant amount of time to travel to weekly therapy sessions, you can still watch instructional videos on YouTube, read books, and ask lots of questions of professionals. I wish I'd had YouTube in those early days. But I'm grateful for what I did have: great books, an outstanding developmental center with caring therapists, and the Holy Spirit to guide me.

The twins' insurances also didn't pay for such things as music therapy, but we are musicians and exposed the twins to music daily. When they were about nine years old, we gave them small guitars and they "played" them in front of the church with their dad. He showed them which string to pluck at which time. This helped them in several ways. They had to listen and pay attention to their dad's signals. It also helped them overcome their fear of being in front of people. Admittedly, to this day, Isaac likes being in the limelight much more than Isaiah. But Isaiah was willing to be up front with his dad and brother.

The twins love music and the Pandora and YouTube iPhone apps. When they're not busy doing other things, they have earphones in their ears and smiles on their faces. Isaiah will ask me if I like that song (he forgets I can't hear it) and adds, "I love Pandora, Mama." As a musician, I'm tickled that he loves music as much as I do. I often wonder if the

earphones have worked as a sort of auditory therapy as well (another treatment). I'll never know. But it's curious to me that they are calm and happy
after they listen to music.

I'm sure professionals who read this bit of advice will cringe. ABA and
other therapies are usually administered by well-paid, expertly trained
professionals. But if the only options are no intervention because of lack
of funding or the best efforts of an attentive parent, which is better? The
Holy Spirit can supernaturally teach us what we need to know. It won't
be perfect.

But then, what about autism is?

Chapter 10

The Doctor Is In—Or Out

*On hearing this, Jesus said, "It is not the healthy
who need a doctor, but the sick."*
—MATTHEW 9:12

If you are a family member living with autism, chances are you've spent
more time in doctors' waiting rooms than exam rooms. And if your
experiences have been anything like mine, you've also struggled to find a
supportive medical community that understands ASD.

Thankfully, things are improving as—unfortunately—the diagnosis
of the condition skyrockets. More doctors are aware of autism and know
what to look for and what questions to ask. However, hospitals and medical providers still have a lot to learn about providing services to the autism
community.

Waiting Rooms and Doctor's Offices

When the twins were infants, I spent many harrowing hours in waiting
rooms while they screamed their lungs out. It was embarrassing for me,
troubling for people waiting with us, and obviously distressing for the
twins themselves. As you can well imagine, their siblings got no joy from
it either. We took turns walking them up and down the halls, jiggling

their car seats or strollers, and praying for peace. (The check-in staff were always relieved to see us leave!)

In the beginning, in Iowa, we had an excellent family doctor who had nine children of his own. He was a younger doctor with a great attitude toward my questions. I've never forgotten his patience and his open-minded attitude toward my parenting choices in terms of vaccinations and diets. I was sad when we had to move away from him. He was a perfect fit for our family.

In Arkansas, I had a more mature, old-school pediatrician. Though he was brilliant, his nursing staff was judgmental indeed. The other doctors in his practice weren't as understanding, and the office staff didn't grasp the reasons I called ahead to make my appointments. I would carefully inform them days in advance about the twins' special anxiety issues so we could avoid lengthy delays in the waiting area. But after we arrived and the minutes dragged on, most of the staff rolled their eyes and whispered about my twins crawling around the waiting room and howling. When I picked the boys up to comfort them, they pummeled me and pulled my hair, kicked me, and bit me. Have you ever tried to calm two screaming hurricanes? If you know autism, you realize that sometimes there's no way to quell the storm. Since the boys were unable to modulate their emotions, there was no end to their screaming, no matter what I did to try to appease them.

But at least their kind doctor listened well and referred me to a well-known developmental pediatrician who specialized in children with attention deficit hyperactivity disorder (ADHD) and other neurological disorders. I was hopeful we'd find some answers for the boys' bizarre behaviors.

The day we arrived at the specialist's office was hot and humid. I'd gotten lost; this was before the advent of GPS and Google Maps. (How did we ever find our way then?) The air-conditioning had gone out in the van and we were all drained and miserable from the hour-long drive in the Arkansas heat.

Once inside the office we waited another hour, with no drinking fountain in sight (in those days, vending machines didn't stock bottled water). Feeling like I was going to pass out, I beat myself up for being so short-sighted. That's another thing living with autism will do—distract a parent to the point of not remembering some of the little things, like bringing sippy cups with water.

Finally, in the examination room, the doctor looked the boys over and observed me forcing them away from the tongue depressors and cotton swabs. He opened one of their charts and started scribbling. "They're twins." He stopped writing and looked up at me. "They're just vying for your attention. You need to spend more one-on-one time with them." He eyed my other wiggly four-year-old son. "That one probably has ADHD. Have you ever had him evaluated?"

Before I could answer, he caught one of the twins trying to bite the other and slapped his hand. I was stunned. The doctor looked at me, realizing his reflex was out of line. "He's just testing you is all. You need to have firm boundaries."

I held my tongue, but what I wanted to do was pull out my parenting résumé. I had spent the past fifteen years raising children—foster kids and my own—and I knew good and well how to discipline and nurture a child. His condescension grated on me, but I was too exhausted to argue.

He referred me to a developmental psychiatrist and said he'd call after her evaluation. "But I'm sure the behaviors stem from their being twins. You need to be more attentive, Mom. Don't do everything with them together. Take them on outings by themselves."

I clenched my jaw shut and literally bit my tongue. *How did he know how much time I spent with my children?* I was a stay-at-home mother who spent plenty of time with the twins, sometimes at the expense of my other children. Their special needs demanded it. If I hadn't been so thirsty and wrung out, I'd have given him a piece of my mind.

Months later (because it takes that long to get an appointment with a specialist), the twins were evaluated by the developmental psychiatrist. During my first meeting with her, I had a list of questions I wanted to ask.

She listened for a bit, answered some of my questions, and then dismissed me to observe the twins individually. When she brought me back into the room, she proceeded to diagnose *me*.

"You're a little obsessive-compulsive. And I think you might even be clinically depressed."

Well, don't you know that won me right over?

Desperate for answers, I brushed off the doctor's comments. I knew this woman held the key to the mystery behind my boys' odd mannerisms and perception of the world. But when she told me the twins had autism, I was stunned. I'd considered many other things—cognitive disability, oppositional defiant disorder, attachment disorder—but autism? What was that? I didn't know anyone with autism.

After the developmental pediatrician received the twins' psychiatric evaluation, he called me at home.

"I received the evaluation from the psychiatrist. Did she discuss the results of her testing with you?"

"Yes," I answered.

"She says that your sons have autism. There's no way someone can raise twin boys with autism. It's too much. You need to consider giving one of them up."

Needless to say, I didn't go back to that doctor—even though he came highly recommended and had won several awards for his work with children with special needs. *Give one of them up? As if they were puppies? How would I choose?* The mere thought disgusted me.

I hung up the phone, slid down the wall and cried. I'm not certain why I cried, but I think I was crying out of anger more than sadness. If I couldn't even get a specialist to support me, how *was* I going to survive parenting these difficult children?

Bedside Manners or the Lack Thereof

I'm often amazed at the bedside manner of some medical professionals. While I understand that most health-care providers are extremely intelligent, I wonder how they can lack certain social graces. It seems that

Exercising a Proper Filter 101 (especially when dealing with parents of children with special needs) should be a required class in medical school.

The tactless psychiatrist and the developmental pediatrician weren't the only doctors whose opinions stunned me. Once when I took the twins to a pediatrician who was filling in for their regular doctor, he said, "You know, I save the lives of preemies every day. But sitting here observing these guys, sometimes I wonder if I'm doing the right thing."

For a doctor to suggest that maybe it would have been better if my sons hadn't survived their premature birth shocked me. From that point on, I never allowed my sons to be examined by that doctor; I also reported him to my regular doctor.

There's a truth that people working with adoptive families should know. We love our adopted children every bit as much as we love our biological children. I never, ever in my heart differentiate between them. In fact, a social worker commented on the special care I gave our twins.

"You act toward them as if you're their real mom," she said as we sat in a ladies' restroom area that had a bench and I held and fed them.

I looked at her. "But I am their real mom. I am the only mom they know."

In 1997, when the twins got chicken pox at the age of two, they didn't just get a few little poxes; they got boils. The boils got infected. They would have been hospitalized, except that their insightful doctor knew that hospitalizing them would be even more problematic. He trusted my ability to care for the boys and get them through this horrible illness. As he was examining the screaming twins, a nurse walked through the office and quipped, "If they had gotten the chicken pox vaccine they wouldn't be going through this."

The vaccine hadn't been approved in the United States until 1995, the year the twins were born. I wasn't the sort of mother to jump on a vaccine bandwagon without first learning how it affected those taking it. And with their developmental delays and constant ear infections, their vaccinations were a bit behind. I felt immense reassurance when I saw my doctor's disgusted reaction to that nurse's comment. He truly got me as a mom and had compassion for my boys and my situation. I am forever grateful to him for having my back that day. It was bad enough to watch my boys suffer; I didn't need the condemnation. What purpose did it serve to say that to me other than to feed her self-righteous attitude? Nursing should be a ministry of compassion and healing, not condemnation.

Tips for Working with the Medical Community

Working with the medical community is another battle families with autism must learn to wage with grace. It certainly isn't easy, and I continue to be challenged in this area. There are some things I wish every clinic and hospital would practice to help families bringing children with autism to them. What follows are a few of my best suggestions for parents. I hope medical professionals will understand them as well.

Find Doctors Who Will Respect and Listen to You

If your doctors refuse to listen, find ones who will. Much of the stress in rearing children with autism comes from not being able to communicate openly with doctors and their staff. I know it's overwhelming, but nip problems in the bud in the beginning of a patient-doctor relationship by finding the right medical professionals. It will reduce stress significantly. Unfortunately, living in a rural area as we do, there were some battles that were hard to fight because my choices were slim. But getting along with their doctors was a series of battles I'm happy to have fought and won.

Do Whatever It Takes to Accommodate Your Child

Never apologize for helping your child feel comfortable in the hospital or clinic. Autism creates high anxiety in children. You know how you feel about having to go to the clinic, right? Imagine that anxiety multiplied by a thousand. There are logical, simple things you can do to help your child cope. I've heard of parents moving favorite rocking chairs from home into hospital rooms to help soothe their children. If that's what it takes, why not?

Help medical personnel understand that the primary emotion for your child is fear. Help alleviate fear of the unknown by using social stories (see chapter 8) so your child will better understand your trips to the doctor or to prepare them for a hospital stay. You may also want to rehearse certain procedures at home beforehand, such as EEGs or EKGs. (I have nightmare stories about the twins' experiences with those.) Have the child practice wearing a hat and putting stickers on it for the EEG preparation. Practice putting stickers on the child's chest and tummy to prepare for the EKG. Also, let them watch YouTube videos about the procedures, as well as handle and feel similar types of wires. My sons were absolutely terrified of all the wires, and the technicians were clueless about autism. I have never felt anger and sympathy toward medical personnel simultaneously until I held my twins in my lap for EKGs! Encourage hospitals to let the child handle the doctor's tools, such as the stethoscope and old, never-to-be-used-again parts of an EEG or EKG machine. Give the child time to explore an IV pole and bag. Familiarity alleviates fear.

Embrace the Familiar
Give medicine in a favorite cup. Bring a favorite toy to hold during exams or blood draws. We started video recording the twins getting blood draws; for some reason that helped them be more brave the next time. You can also practice putting on hospital gowns and hospital armbands at home before a hospital stay.

Speak Up!
Ask the doctor if each test is absolutely necessary for a diagnosis. Sometimes tests are redundant. While it's important to remember that you may not have a degree in medicine, sometimes medical staff do things routinely that can be otherwise skipped.

Also, ask if it's absolutely necessary for the child to spend the night. One of our boys had an implant in his eyelid muscle that erupted. When we took him to the emergency room, they wanted to put him on an IV all night. I knew that we'd be up all night, fighting him. Instead, we asked if we could take him home as long as we promised not to feed him anything until surgery the next day. Thankfully, they agreed. They simply hadn't thought of that option.

It's also important to educate professionals about your child's triggers. One of the best ways to do this is to prepare a care notebook to take with you to appointments. The American Academy of Pediatrics has a fantastic website with printable forms for you to use for building one. You can find this resource at www.medicalhomeinfo.org or http://cshcn. org/planning-record-keeping/care-organizer-for-parents/ (or google "care notebook"). These are some of the things you may want to include in your notebook:

- What things are upsetting to your child.
- What things calm your child (if anything).
- How your child reacts to sedation. One of my boys shocked hospital staff when they gave him medication to make him sleepy before putting in his IV for surgery. Even though I told them it wouldn't put him to sleep, they didn't believe me. Sure enough, they ended up carrying a screaming, terrified child to the operating room.
- Whether your child prefers male or female staff.
- How much time the doctor(s) can anticipate in examining the child (depending on your child's level of cooperation).
- How your child communicates (especially if they are nonverbal) and how your medical team can communicate each action before it occurs to help alleviate fear of the unknown.
- Whether your child will allow someone to touch them, such as on the hand or the top of the head.
- Whether your child may do better with one consistent doctor or nurse instead of a plethora of folks wandering in and out. This is especially important for teaching hospitals to know as student doctors often stop in with other doctors to observe.
- Your child's sleeping habits (children with autism often do not sleep well).
- Your child's medications—including times of day taken and amount.

Also, list those medications your child is allergic to or other allergies your child may have, such as bee stings or lotions or soaps.

- Blank pages for questions, with space left for answers you may receive.
- Phone numbers for the pharmacy and other doctors and specialists, including therapists.
- School information.
- Nutrition, including any food allergies and times of day your child needs to eat. If your child is rigid in their meal routines, let the staff know, and be firm in your request to have their tray sent to their room at a specific time.
- Lighting preferences. What kind of lighting will help your child remain calm? Are bright lights difficult? Ask that they be dimmed.
- Anything else you want to include in the notebook or feel the doctor should know. It's your child's notebook and it won't look like someone else's.

ER Stories

I raised four boys, and for a season it seemed as if I was in the emergency room at least once a week. It's not always possible to prepare for an emergency, but I definitely suggest taking helpers along to the ER. Recruit a neighbor if you must. One of my most memorable trips to the emergency room was when Isaiah got a huge splinter in his foot. It was too deep for us to get to it. For some reason, that day my husband and I were alone with the twins. When it came time for the doctor to take out the splinter, three male nurses wrapped Isaiah up like a burrito in a blanket. It took them and my husband to hold him down while the doctor pulled the splinter out.

In the meantime, I was all alone with the other twin, Isaac, who refused to be distracted. He could hear his brother screaming and was doing everything in his power to get to Isaiah. Isaac himself was screaming and crying, terrified about what was happening to his brother. The twins have always had an almost supernatural strength, and my arms ached from holding on to Isaac to keep him from running into the exam room. People in the waiting area stared as I tried to distract him with the lobby's fish tank, but Isaac would have none of it.

"Want my bruddah!"

I still remember his red, indignant little face. He was furious. In his nine-year-old mind, those men were hurting his brother and it was his job to rescue him.

Another incident occurred in a lab waiting area where I was supposed to somehow make the four-year-old boys (who were not yet potty trained) pee into a cup. Needless to say, that didn't happen. That test got skipped.

Learning to forge your way through the medical system takes the bravery of Joan of Arc and the tenacity of a pit bull. The hardest part, I think, is learning to do it with grace. I've learned I make much more progress when working with professionals by being less frantic and more appreciative. It's sort of like playing a chess game. I sit back, observe, and listen before I make my move. This is where wisdom comes in. Neither parents nor doctors are all-knowing. But as Christian parents, we have a relationship with the One who is omniscient.

"Let your gentleness be evident to all. The Lord is near. Do not be anxious about anything, but in every situation, by prayer and petition, with thanksgiving, present your requests to God. And the peace of God, which transcends all understanding, will guard your hearts and your minds in Christ Jesus" (Phil. 4:5–7).

Chapter II

Diets, Vaccines, and Medications

One person considers one day more sacred than another;
another considers every day alike. Each of them should be
fully convinced in their own mind.

—ROMANS 14:5

If I had a dime for every time someone approached me with a cure for my twins' autism, I'd be able to fund enough research to discover one. Well, okay, maybe I wouldn't have that much money, but it does happen a lot.

"Did you know that if you stop feeding your children gluten, they will be cured?"

"I just heard on a talk show that if you cut dairy out of your kids' diets, the autism will go away."

"If you cleanse their bodies of the heavy metal toxins they got from vaccines when they were babies, they'll start talking."

These are just a few of the many, many "cures" that well-meaning friends and acquaintances have tried to get me to use. The thing is, we'd already tried the diet route. For my boys, diet wasn't the cause of their autism. Eliminating gluten, dairy, and many other foods brought no results.

That doesn't mean it doesn't work for some children. I know several families whose children did improve with a change in diet, but they weren't *cured*. Not all children's autism is caused by food intolerances or allergies. My sons have chronic problems, including fetal alcohol spectrum disorders, intellectual disabilities, and speech and language disorders. A change in diet won't cure all that. Their behavior stems from brain abnormalities rather than the flora in their gut.

Countless so-called treatments and therapies claim to help children recover from autism. I've watched too many families mortgage their homes and go into debt to pay for treatments that bring their child no more results than a developmental preschool would provide. It's not that I blame the parents. Every good parent will move heaven and earth to help their child. We want to fix what's wrong. But I do blame the charlatans who claim their therapies are the best cure and milk vulnerable parents out of thousands of dollars.

So What Really Works for My Family?

Since all children with autism have unique brains, symptoms, and outcomes, it's hard to pinpoint one best method of treating this puzzling disorder. And therein lies the problem. It takes wisdom on the part of the parent to choose an appropriate therapy or treatment. Prayer is a tremendous tool, since God knows our child's needs much better than we do. And he can show us which road to take. He doesn't want us to be tricked.

"Trust in the LORD with all your heart and lean not on your own understanding; in all your ways submit to him, and he will make your paths straight" (Prov. 3:5–6).

Before committing to an expensive treatment program, pray. A lot. Then talk to other parents about what they're using and outcomes they've experienced. Remember, you don't want a treatment that makes you feel good about yourself, but one that produces results for your child. Another thing to consider is how much time it will take away from being a family, especially if you have typical children growing up in the home too.

When I was driving an hour each way to therapies several times a week,

I had to reevaluate what it was doing to us as a family unit. Our lives were revolving around treatments instead of one another. I had to make the decision to modify our plan in everyone's best interests. It was one of the best decisions I ever made.

Another thing to keep in mind is that there are some therapies and treatments that "cross over." Some doctors and therapists use a little of the best from each method; I actually prefer this approach. Why not use the finest of each to create a well-rounded outcome? There are no perfect therapies or treatments. Each has strengths and weaknesses. Being puritanical about a particular method could shortchange your child's progress.

One way to decide which treatment might work best is to study their efficacy. Investigate the claims of each. What has research shown regarding the outcome? How is it measured? Are there risks? What are the benefits? What results do you desire for your child? Will this therapy or treatment point your child toward this end? Just because a treatment is appealing or fun doesn't mean it works. To do your homework, type "efficacy and [autism treatment]" into a search engine and read up before deciding. In this way, you won't be tricked by shiny flash-in-the-pan trends. Unfortunately, there are plenty of people out there willing to take your hard-earned money. It's a shameful truth in the disability community.

Whatever you prayerfully choose, ignore the opinions of self-proclaimed experts who try to influence your decision or plant doubts in your mind. There are several opposing camps out there who claim they have the best and only answers. Instead of uniting the autism community, they've created a deep divide. Even nonprofit organizations have been known to strive against each other. If an organization or method is forcefully vocal and critical of other parents' choices or therapies, it makes me suspicious. What are they afraid of? What do they have to gain by being negative? If their primary interest is steering folks toward their therapy or organization for financial gain, that's a definite red flag.

We serve a God of great wisdom. He will give you the discernment to choose wisely. You need only ask: "Dear friends, do not believe every spirit, but test the spirits to see whether they are from God, because many false prophets have gone out into the world" (1 John 4:1).

Just as there are false prophets in Christendom, there are false prophets in the autism community. Someone who claims to have the only answer or cure? I would be suspicious. Autism is unique to every child. The results of treatment will produce unique, individual results.

Some organizations choose opinionated celebrities as their spokespeople. I find it best to ignore such "expertise." For one thing, these folks are usually out of touch with mainstream families and are able to access therapies and treatments that charge exorbitant amounts of money—more money than most of us make in a lifetime. For another thing, the fact that it works for their child doesn't mean it's a cure for all children. This is what puzzles me most. If you are truly an advocate for autism, you will campaign for all children and families, not just an elite few. Don't divide the autism community into us and them or make an already bewildering issue even more confusing.

To make things even more perplexing, there's a camp that says parents are wrong to fight against autism. Made up mostly of adults with a diagnosis of autism, this group believes parents should accept the disorder as it is and embrace it, because autism isn't a disorder but a different way of being. They believe that treating autism destroys the personality of the child and that it's the neurologically typical who need treatment, not those with autism.

The irony of this outlook is that these advocates are clearly able to communicate their point of view. Nonverbal people with autism are not. To be such outspoken advocates, they probably had therapy or treatment that got them where they are today in terms of communication—or they were born with a much milder diagnosis.

Other camps include the gluten-free and casein-free camp, the anti-vaccine camp, the vitamin-and-supplement camp, the anti-psychotropic-drugs camp, and many, many more. In fact, whatever treatment, diet, or therapy you choose, there will be those who oppose it. And for every treatment plan you don't subscribe to, there will be people who will criticize you for using a different one. This is frustrating and discouraging. Instead of tearing each other down, we need to hold each other up. If we don't help one another, we can't expect anyone outside of the autism community to care.

Treatments range from swimming with dolphins to riding motorcycles to soaking in the Dead Sea. While these are fun activities, I'm not sure there is data to support them as proven outcome-based therapies. I admit that working with our pets has helped the twins tremendously in terms of wanting to interact. Riding with us on our motorcycles continues to have a calming effect on them. But these experiences are only a small part of a bigger treatment plan that has contributed to their progress and ability to communicate today.

Our family's "radical" approach to treating our boys was to read up on everything and integrate elements of the ones that made sense into our daily lives. We believed (and still do) that children with autism must be meaningfully engaged as often as possible. It's too easy to allow them to sit in front of their favorite television programs or to play video games. And while we did allow such activities, we're thankful our busy lifestyle limited them.

Cure or Quackery?

Recently the Food and Drug Administration (FDA) cracked down on companies who claim to cure autism. These companies market such treatments as hyperbaric oxygen therapy, chelation therapies and detoxifying clay baths, probiotics and coconut kefir, and Miracle Mineral Solution (MMS). These are just a few of the treatments that tout cures without verifiable evidence.

Hyperbaric Oxygen Therapy

Hyperbaric oxygen therapy is performed in a pressurized chamber. It's a valid treatment used for certain medical problems, such as decompression sickness suffered by divers or those exposed to carbon monoxide. It hasn't been approved by the FDA for treating autism and there is no verifiable data to prove it works. Parents choose this treatment because it claims to remove toxins (think heavy metals), reduce inflammation, and allow greater blood flow to oxygen-deprived areas of the body. It's also believed to build new capillaries in the brain and reduce inflammation in the gut. The danger of this treatment is that it can induce seizures and release excess oxygen into the central nervous system and bloodstream.

Chelation
Chelation therapies claim to cleanse the body of toxic chemicals and heavy metals. Parents turn to this treatment because they believe their child's autistic symptoms are caused by the presence of heavy metals that entered their child's body via vaccines. This therapy is applied through the use of sprays, pills, drops, suppositories, or clay baths. Chelation is used to treat lead poisoning and iron overload, but the medications for this are only available by prescription and under the supervision of a medical doctor. The danger of chelation is that it can remove minerals the body needs. For example, calcium is depleted during chelation, which can cause the heart to stop. Children have died undergoing such procedures! There's an increase in nonprescription products that claim to rid the body of heavy metals and toxic chemicals, thereby curing autism. However, these claims are not supported by scientific evidence.

Probiotics
Coconut kefir and other probiotics are just a few of many natural supplements touted as a cure for autism. As of this writing, I've never used coconut kefir specifically and don't know anyone who has. I do take a probiotic myself and experience positive effects from doing so. My sons take one, but I've not seen their autism cured as a result. It's the claims of an autism cure that the FDA takes issue with.

Miracle Mineral Solution
Miracle Mineral Solution, also known as Miracle Mineral Supplement, Master Mineral Solution, or MMS, is a product that becomes a potent

chemical when mixed according to package directions. The FDA reports that consumers have experienced nausea, severe vomiting, and life-threatening low blood pressure after drinking an MMS and citrus juice mixture. It released an alert in 2010, warning consumers not to take MMS because, when used as directed, it can cause serious harm to health.

MMS is a toxic solution of distilled water and sodium chlorite—the same ingredients in industrial-strength bleach. There is a diluted version marketed as Chlorine Dioxide Solution.

The inventor of MMS claims it's a cure for cancer, autism, HIV, malaria, hepatitis viruses, cold viruses, and acne. It's sometimes sold as a water purifier to avoid regulation. Parents travel to Mexico to so-called clinics where their children receive enemas with this solution. The protocol calls for MMS to sit in the colon for twelve to thirty minutes. This is performed several times a week. They also soak children in hot baths (as warm as they can tolerate) of the solution. Another way they apply the treatment is to add it to their child's citrus drinks.

The results of MMS treatments are often diarrhea and vomiting along with a fever. Proponents call it "fever therapy," claiming it's the body's way of waking up the immune system and getting rid of not only parasites but other toxins that may cause autism.

Other Controversial Treatments

There are many more unproven treatments that profess to cure autism but have no empirical scientific evidence to back up their claims: stem cell therapy, secretin injections, antifungal agent therapy, raw camel's milk, marijuana therapy, nicotine patch therapy, transcranial magnetic stimulation (TMS), holding therapy, prism glasses, and more. Do a search on the Internet and you'll find all sorts of unproven treatments, ranging from exorcism to chemical castration.

Chemical castration is a so-called cure introduced by a father-son doctor team, Mark and David Geier. In simple terms, their hypothesis is that testosterone contributes to autism by binding with mercury from vaccines. In order for them to use a drug called Lupron (used to chemically

castrate sex offenders), they "diagnose" children with autism with preco-
cious puberty. Harmful side effects include hives, difficulty breathing and
swallowing, testicular pain, painful urination, and more.

Exorcism has been used by more families than I care to acknowledge.
Now, I'm a true believer in prayer, faith, and healing. But for a child with
autism to be held down and prayed over for hours must be harrowing. I
can't imagine having someone do that to me. Children have died after
being wrapped in blankets and held down during prayer services. There
is no example of this in Scripture. When Jesus cast out demons, he didn't
hold anyone down and it didn't take hours.

Guidelines for Choosing Treatments

My heart breaks especially for children with severe forms of autism who
can't speak for themselves. It's upsetting to know that parents not only go
to such lengths to pay for such treatments, but risk their children's lives
in the reckless pursuit of hope. This is why we must base our decisions
on evidence, rather than on emotions and anecdotal claims. Testimonials
aren't enough.

So how does one choose? Here are a few guidelines to help:

- Search for evidence-based treatments that have been thoroughly
  investigated and show measurable improvements in targeted areas.
- Studies should include well-matched comparison groups. Ideally,
  those receiving the intervention should be compared to those receiving no intervention or standard interventions.
- The two comparison groups should match in gender distribution,
  age, level of functioning, diagnosis, and any other applicable characteristics.
- Variables should be recognized and taken into consideration.
- Measurements should be given before and after the study.
- To prevent bias, those participating in the study—parents, children,
  and investigators—shouldn't know which group they are in.
- You can find many autism research topics on the Autism Science

Foundation website (autismsciencefoundation.org). Look for the toolkit to download a list of resources regarding autism research.

If you choose to use an unproven treatment, do so carefully. Vitamin supplements are beneficial for most people to maintain a healthy and balanced diet. But when they are misused, they can be toxic, especially when taken in high doses. Diet is important as well, but be careful that your child is getting enough calcium and nutrients for healthy bones if using the dairy-free or gluten- and casein-free diets. And remember, these are not cures. It's one thing to use them to improve your child's quality of life and quite another to expect a cure.

I have a dear friend who has three children on the autism spectrum. She feeds her family an all-organic, gluten-free diet. She is an excellent mother and her children are extremely healthy because of the vigilance she pays to their diet. I think every parent has a strength they bring to their children when it comes to treatments. For some parents it's a pure diet; for others it may be education. Whichever path a parent chooses, that's between them and the Lord and not for others to judge.

Which treatments are backed by empirical evidence? None. Well, none that cure autism. But there are well-studied treatments with proven evidence for facilitating progress.

Medication

There are only two medications that have been approved by the FDA for the treatment of autism. The first is Risperidone, which is approved for the treatment of symptoms associated with ASD in children and adolescents. Risperidone helps with aggressive behavior, self-injury, and temper tantrums. The second drug approved by the FDA is Aripiprazole, used to treat irritability. As with any drug, both have side effects, so parents should use caution. Weigh them carefully when considering either drug, or any other kind of psychotropic drug.

Other medications may be suggested by your child's doctor that have been successful for children and adolescents with autism but have not yet published studies to prove their efficacy. Stay informed by reading about the research and side effects. Consider accessing treatment through clinicians specializing in autism alone. We were blessed to use the Christian Sarkine Autism Treatment Center at Riley Children's Hospital in Indianapolis for nearly fifteen years. Now that the twins are adults, I miss that time with the center and the doctor who helped us navigate the world of psychotropic medications. We were blessed indeed to make our journey there.

Vaccines

Another treatment issue that comes up frequently for all families, but especially those with autism, is the question of vaccines. Should or shouldn't we vaccinate? Do vaccines cause autism? These questions deeply divide the medical and autism communities.

Those who support vaccines argue that no one has the right to risk public health for moral, philosophical, or religious reasons. They believe that vaccines prevent serious diseases that were known to kill thousands of children, such as polio and smallpox. According to the Pediatric Academic Society, childhood vaccinations in the United States prevent nearly eleven million cases of infectious illness and thirty-three thousand deaths per year.[1] According to the American Academy of Pediatrics, childhood vaccines are 90 to 99 percent effective in preventing diseases, and if a child does get the disease in spite of being vaccinated, they have much milder symptoms.[2] Not vaccinating children puts the population at risk. To achieve herd immunity, 75 to 94 percent of the population must be vaccinated. Only when this is achieved is the prevention of the spread of disease accomplished.

Preventable diseases, such as mumps and measles, can cause permanent disabilities and even death. In 1991, seven children in Philadelphia died of measles; mumps can cause deafness. Even though a very small number of deaths from the measles, mumps, and rubella (MMR) vaccine have been reported, the most common reactions are fever and minor soreness.

The pro-vaccine camp emphatically denies that vaccines cause autism.

On March 12, 2010, in the case of *Mead v. Secretary of Health and Human Services*,[3] the United States Court of Federal Claims ruled that the theory that vaccines cause autism is scientifically unsupportable. The Centers for Disease Control and Prevention (CDC) also believes that vaccines should be required for economic reasons. Every dollar spent on vaccines saves society $10.10 in medical costs.[4]

Those who oppose vaccines dispute these claims and don't believe the government has the right to intervene in decisions parents make for their children's health. Others have religious objections to vaccines and believe that forcing them on their children is a violation of their First Amendment rights.

Some believe vaccines are unnecessary in many cases because the threat of death or disability from the disease is small. They also believe that many childhood diseases, such as whooping cough, measles, and scarlet fever, had already decreased before vaccines due to improved water, sewage treatment, and nutrition.

Some parents who oppose vaccinations believe they cause severe reactions, including autism, ADHD, death, and autoimmune disorders—such as arthritis, multiple sclerosis, lupus, fibromyalgia, Guillain-Barré syndrome, and others. Some also believed that vaccines disrupt the lymphatic system and can lead to lymphatic cancers. When they weigh the risk of the diseases against the adverse effects of the vaccine, they choose to risk the diseases because most are not life-threatening. They feel that vaccines damage the natural immune system and that unvaccinated children build up and strengthen their immune systems by developing natural immunities to such diseases as measles and chicken pox.

Another compelling argument against vaccines is that many of the members of the CDC Advisory Committee on Immunization Practices are those with significant financial ties to vaccine companies. For example, the American Academy of Pediatrics, a leader in pro-vaccination propaganda, receives millions of dollars from vaccine companies.[5]

The dramatic rise in the number of vaccinations for a child under the age of six is another reason some parents are unwilling to vaccinate. In

1950, children only received seven vaccines by the age of six. In 1980, the number of vaccines was ten. Now the CDC schedule requires a child to receive thirty-six vaccines before the age of six. It is no wonder parents correlate the rise of autism with the rise of vaccines.

Lastly, many have religious objections to vaccines because components of some were developed from the cells of human fetuses. The abortions of these fetuses weren't conducted for vaccine production, but the idea that the cultures originated from these babies is repugnant. The vaccines that use WI-38 cell strain developed in the United States in 1961 and the MRC-5 cell strain developed in 1965 in the United Kingdom are the following:

- Hepatitis A vaccines [VAQTA/Merck, Havrix/GlaxoSmithKline, and part of Twinrix/GlaxoSmithKline]
- Rubella vaccine [MERUVAX II/Merck, part of MMR II/Merck, and ProQuad/Merck]
- Varicella (chicken pox) vaccine [Varivax/Merck and part of ProQuad/Merck]
- Zoster (shingles) vaccine [Zostavax/Merck]
- Adenovirus Type 4 and Type 7 oral vaccine [Barr Labs]
- Rabies vaccine [IMOVAX/Sanofi Pasteur][6]

Vaccination is an extremely personal decision, and just as you'll need prayerful guidance when making such a choice, you should also carefully review the evidence. Where you live, your lifestyle, and personal beliefs should be considered. If you choose not to vaccinate, you'll need to take appropriate steps for exemption when enrolling your child in public school. If you choose to vaccinate, be well informed of the consequences and options that are available in terms of the vaccination schedule and dosage.

Whatever your decision, know there is a Great Physician who is bigger than any disease or adverse reaction. When you ask God to show you which interventions to choose and access, I have great faith to believe he will show you. And once that decision is made, live with it, in the belief that God is up to something good.

Don't judge others who make choices different from your own. God gave their children to them, not to you. What anyone decides is between them and God. Leave everyone else in his wonderful hands and focus on your own matters.

As Christian parents, especially, we must be there for each other and hold each other up on this blinding, confusing road of treatments. We need each other. United we can do much more than we can divided. The world is watching us. What do they see? Let's hope they watch biblical wisdom in action, such as:

> Therefore encourage one another and build each other up, just as in fact you are doing. (1 Thess. 5:11)

> If one part suffers, every part suffers with it; if one part is honored, every part rejoices with it. (1 Cor. 12:26)

> Rejoice with those who rejoice; mourn with those who mourn. (Rom. 12:15)

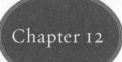

Chapter 12

Public, Private, or Homeschool?

*For the LORD gives wisdom; from his mouth come
knowledge and understanding.*
—PROVERBS 2:6

Before you read this chapter, you should know that I come from a long line of educators.

My ancestors built the first one-room schoolhouse in Halifax, Pennsylvania. My father is a retired public school teacher and I've taught in private schools, as well as homeschooled my children. I'm a public shool teacher and have a degree in special education and a doctorate in Christian education, so I arrive at this issue with experience and a passionate love for all things academic. My kids often tell their friends, "My mom has been in school my entire life. She's always studying something."

It's true. I love books, school supplies, technology, writing papers, and learning new things. There's just about nothing I enjoy more than satisfying my own curiosity and piquing it in my students. That joke about reading the entire Internet? I've actually tried to do that.

Parents are as passionate about their school choices for their children as they are about treatments. As I mentioned before, we should respect one another's decisions and decide what's best for our own children. What's best for someone else's child is their business because God gave their child to them, not you.

Our twins have attended all three types of school: public, private, and homeschool. Our choices for them at different times in their lives were based on their needs and our family's needs. My husband and I arrived at our choices through much prayer and careful thought. It was never easy, but looking back, I regret none of our decisions. Again, our choices will not match yours because your child is unique and so is your family. With all this in mind, here's our story.

Developmental Preschool

It didn't feel right to wake up my two-and-a-half-year-old sons for an hour-long ride to the all-day program at Sunshine School, a developmental preschool center for children with special needs. The first weeks were difficult for me and caused me to question my commitment to homeschooling as the best method of educating our children. Still, I knew I didn't have all the answers for my boys and I needed to get them help. Sunshine was the best option for them at this time.

Every day for weeks they screamed in terror as we placed them in their car seats on the school van. I knew they were well cared for because I kept close tabs on them by visiting the preschool frequently and staying in touch with the staff. They were assigned a caseworker who helped me advocate for any services they qualified for, as well as navigate the mounds of paperwork involved.

I cried those first weeks. A lot. It rubbed me the wrong way as a mother to let them go. I was a staunch homeschool advocate for spiritual reasons. Even though my father hadn't agreed with my homeschool choice (he was, after all, a public school teacher), homeschooling was what I believed God wanted for my other children.

As a homeschooling parent, I prayed every single year (sometimes daily) about my school choices for my children. Who in their right mind wants to keep their kids home when a big yellow bus could swallow them up each day and give the mother six-plus hours of freedom? Or the chance for a career of her own? Apparently me. I loved every second with my children. Don't get me wrong; homeschooling wasn't all butterflies and unicorns. There were very hard days when I didn't like doing it. Still, I believed I was obeying God in my school choice for my other children, and that's why they were at home.

I also feel that the twins being at Sunshine School those two years was good for my other kids. It gave us time without the chaotic screaming and light flipping, and gave all of us peace, space, and time to think. Not that we didn't all adore the twins. And not that we didn't miss them. I think I'm the one who missed them the most, but now I had time and freedom to take my other children to the library or museum without wrestling two escape artists.

Thankfully, in time, the twins grew to love the ride to school, and the therapists commented to me that the journey seemed to calm and organize their brains. This was before the twins were on any medications other than vitamin supplements. They were extremely busy, anxious little fellows. By the time they got to school, they were able to sit for a while, at least long enough to get through breakfast without a meltdown. I still smile remembering how they would sign "bus" when I woke them up. (Even though it was a van, we called it the bus.)

Public School

After we moved from Arkansas to Indiana, it was a huge disappointment not to find another Sunshine School. Instead there was only a developmental preschool offered through the public school system that met three hours a day, four days a week. I was devastated. How could the boys possibly make progress with so little intervention?

The teachers were wonderful, but as I explained in chapter 5, they weren't aware of the same tools that we used in Arkansas. Sign language wasn't used either, which left me in a state of panic.

And angry.

Looking back, I probably didn't handle things as gracefully as I should have. I wish I could go back and do it over again. I had been spoiled at Sunshine School because I never had to worry that the twins were missing out on an intervention because it was provided so seamlessly, with an integrated approach. All day. Five days a week.

The Indiana preschool was definitely an enriching experience for the boys. And the teachers were bubbly, energetic, and kind. They were using what they'd been given to use and following standard policies and procedures. I don't blame them. I fault a system that moves painfully slowly. By the time changes and improvements occur, the child is graduating from high school.

The twins moved on to all-day kindergarten and they had two of the best teachers on the planet. By this time, I'd pretty much resigned myself to the fact that the school wasn't interested in any of my ideas or how things had been done elsewhere. The twins lost almost all of their sign language (I used it, but the boys wouldn't) and only used pictures at home.

They attended all-day kindergarten two years in a row, and their extremely dedicated teachers went the extra mile and helped them to potty train. This was huge for us, of course, and I was grateful for how the boys progressed. They also had a wonderful male special education teacher who constantly thought of new ways to keep the twins engaged when they were in his classroom for special instruction. Their favorite game was to fish for the alphabet with a fishing pole he bought for them.

In first grade, things changed. The academic challenges were greater and I began to see that the twins' inclusion in a regular classroom wasn't serving them well. Plus, they were being sent home with homework they clearly couldn't do on their own. Because it was school policy, they had to do it. No matter how much I tried to address this issue in their IEP meetings, the teachers and school administrators didn't seem to understand and the meaningless homework kept coming home.

If the twins didn't do their homework, they were punished the next day by being kept inside for recess. This was the last thing these wiggly little boys needed. If their homework wasn't completed, it was because I couldn't get them to cooperate to complete it the evening before. They worked so hard to hold it together at school that in the evening they simply fell apart. They were too emotionally exhausted to sit and do homework they couldn't understand.

In spite of this frustration, the twins learned to form short, two- to three-word sentences and somehow learned to read phonetically. Both boys progressed in reading at the same speed. However, in math they were completely lost. But it wasn't their academic progress I was concerned about. It was their social skills that I felt weren't being addressed, as well as their language skills.

I began to pray about God's will for the twins' second grade year. I wanted to be positively sure that God wanted me to teach them. I didn't want to assume in any way that I had all the answers. I truly needed the Lord to show me which way to go. It was an agonizing decision.

It's that way for all parents. I have friends whose children are in less-than-ideal programs because that's all that's available in rural Indiana. I can't help but wonder what would happen if children with disabilities were given the best programs, without discrimination because of location. Many other parents must settle for the mediocre because they don't know that there are alternatives.

School Choice Comparisons

There are advantages and disadvantages to any program. Here are the advantages and disadvantages of public, private, and home education as I see it.

PUBLIC SCHOOL

Advantages
- Free and appropriate
- Free transportation
- Access to speech therapy on-site
- Access to occupational therapy on-site
- Access to physical therapy on-site
- Licensed general education teachers
- Licensed special education teachers
- Free lunches if student qualifies

- More extracurricular activities, such as sports, music, and art
- Parent gets a break from caregiving
- Child may develop friendships
- By law must provide an IEP for child with disabilities
- May have better facilities
- More choices of classes
- Builds community relationships for parents and students
- School accountable to the state

Disdvantages
- School offers only "free and appropriate," meaning that by law they do not have to provide free and best
- Must attend zoned school, thereby limiting choice
- Exposure to values that are contrary to family or religious beliefs
- Exposure to drugs, sexual promiscuity, and violence
- Higher risk of bullying
- Less one-on-one instruction due to class size
- Less individualized attention and supervision throughout the day if school refuses to provide an aide
- Risk of getting lost in the shuffle
- Too much emphasis on standardized testing
- Student culture can be overwhelming for children with autism
- Less opportunity for child to pursue individual interests or fascinations
- Teachers must teach to tests, thereby limiting time for creative activities
- Academic skills are the focus and training in social skills is secondary (students with autism need just as much opportunity to learn appropriate social skills as algebra)
- Less independent learning

PRIVATE SCHOOL

Advantages
- Small class size
- More one-on-one instruction
- More attention to individual needs
- Child develops friendships
- Less probability of exposure to values different from parents' values
- Less probability of violence, bullying, and drugs

- School can modify curriculum to meet child's needs (if they are willing)
- Teachers are more likely to interact with parents
- More opportunities for unique experiences, such as field trips or projects

Disadvantages
- Tuition costs
- Books and supplies costs
- Mealtime costs (no free lunches)
- Teachers may not be licensed
- Are not required to provide special education on-site
- May not provide an IEP
- Fewer choices in subjects/classes
- Child may not attend school with neighborhood friends

HOMESCHOOL

Advantages
- One-on-one instruction
- More attention to individual needs
- Parent in control of schedule
- Less stress for parent due to not battling with school bureaucracy
- More time for therapies and treatments
- Educational freedom: choice to learn and study what they want, when they want, where they want
- Life can revolve around family schedule instead of school schedule, providing opportunities for out-of-town trips during the school year
- More time for extracurricular activities, such as music lessons, sports, field trips, and more
- Freedom from need to fit in
- Religious freedom
- More predictability for child with special needs and thereby less stress
- Well-rested students
- No busywork or meaningless homework
- Values of family reinforced
- Less time sitting at a desk

Disadvantages
- Parent never gets a break from caregiving unless they advocate for it
- Parent must determine curriculum and implement it

- Parent does all the instruction, therapy, and social skills training
- More stress for parent because all responsibility for child's education is on their shoulders
- Less free family time
- Cost of all curriculum, books, and therapy supplies paid for by parents
- Less social interaction with others
- Isolation and loneliness
- Parent may experience burnout
- Less structure
- Not as many opportunities to practice social skills with those outside the family

My husband and I attended the twins' second-grade IEP meeting (held in the spring in order to plan for the fall) and listened carefully to every person at the table. We wanted to make our decision based on facts, not emotion. There was still no attempt by the school to address the need for more attention to social skills and language experiences. And while inclusion was appreciated, we knew the boys needed more individual attention than what they offered in second grade.

After the meeting, we took their special education teacher aside and shared our concerns. We wanted him to know what we were considering and how very much we appreciated his hard work. He completely understood and gave us his blessing in whatever we decided. I've never forgotten his kindness to us and the twins (especially in the beginning when he was the recipient of a few firm bites from the boys).

I solidified my decision during an end-of-the-year picnic at Isaiah's teacher's house. Children mingled and played together, but Isaiah sat alone on a blanket while I helped pass out drinks. No one approached him to say hello or seemed to notice he was there. It was then that I knew without a doubt that bringing the twins home for school was the right thing to do.

Only, we weren't exactly bringing them home.

Chapter 13

Little Cottage School on the Prairie

Start children off on the way they should go, and even
when they are old they will not turn from it.
—PROVERBS 22:6

The twins weren't the only ones I was bringing home for school. After homeschooling their entire lives, my other two sons had spent the past school year at a private Christian academy while I took a position at a social services organization. But the school was a forty-minute drive each way and costly. Clearly God was stirring my nest and had other things in mind.

After I prayed, researched, and wrestled with my own will, God made it clear. After several parents approached me about their desire for their children to attend a homeschool-style school, I decided to take a plunge of faith and start a cottage school at our church.

The Charlotte Mason Philosophy

The homeschooling philosophy I embraced as a young mother was the Charlotte Mason method. Charlotte Mason was an educator in the late

1800s who believed that parents should educate the whole person, not just the mind. It wasn't until I started educating the twins myself that I discovered how beautifully this philosophy worked for children with special needs. In Mason's words, "Education is an atmosphere, a discipline, a life."[1]

In this method, it is believed that the ideas that rule your life as a parent make up one-third of your child's education. Discipline that cultivates good habits, another third. And, finally, life—as applied to academics—should be presented to children as living thoughts and ideas, not dry facts.

Living methods meant that instead of using textbooks we used "living books." These are usually written in a narrative or story form by an author who has a passion for their topic and makes the subject come alive. This method also requires students to tell back or narrate what has been read to secure it in their minds. Worksheets with fill-in-the-blanks or multiple-choice questions are limited. Instead, students write what they know or tell what they know. Handwriting and spelling are taught from passages of great books that communicate ideas rather than a list of words out of context.

This method exposes students to great artists and composers, helping students learn to identify their works. Time outdoors is stressed to learn about God's creation firsthand. The Mason method also nurtures habits of attention, best effort, and learning for the joy of learning.

One-Room Cottage School

Our one-room type school opened with ages preschool through twelfth grade. There were two homeschool seniors, including my oldest son, who needed to prepare for college. And there were four-year-olds whose parents wanted them to have a Christian preschool experience. The grades in between were made up of children who, for various reasons, needed an alternative learning environment. At our highest enrollment, we had fifteen students. Preschoolers attended three mornings a week.

I recruited several friends to help me with the school, including Miss Mary, the twins' Sunday school teacher. It was under Miss Mary's tutelage that the twins continued to develop academic skills. But it was the size of our little academy that benefited all the students. They ate lunch at the same time and had recesses together. This interaction between ages helped tremendously in teaching them social skills. Students and teachers went on field trips every other Friday. We visited museums, attended plays, ate out at restaurants to practice our manners, and more. On the Fridays we didn't go on field trips, we often went to Salamonie Forest to work on our nature journals or had a special day at school.

Nature studies were a big emphasis. All ages studied flora and fauna on their own level. Our nature journals included poems of what we were studying, as well as pressed flowers, leaves, and grasses. In the classroom each year I chose a group of animals to focus on (such as birds or insects or mammals) and searched for them in the woods. I read noted author Thornton Burgess's animal books aloud and we studied the wildlife in those stories in depth.

One year we explored North American birds, the next year water animals, and another year woodland animals. Each year we studied a different group of God's creatures. Nothing delighted me more than when my special-needs students picked up caterpillars and beetles with hands that normally refused to touch unfamiliar items because of the texture. I bought jars made especially for observing small creatures and gave one to each student. Other things I provided were magnifying glasses, little nets for catching flying bugs, and lots of hand-sized nature guidebooks for identifying what they studied.

The twins were obsessed with baby frogs, and whenever they found one I allowed them to bring it into the classroom. I have a cute picture of one sitting on a chessboard. (Chess was another frequent activity in our school.) Sadly, one frog got lost in the church and we never did find it. I still wonder where it ended up.

I chose a historical time period as the spine of our school year. The first year we studied ancient history, the next the medieval era, then colonial times, and then on to modern history. Everything we did that school year revolved around and tied into that theme. Our cooking classes, art, books I read aloud, and field trips correlated with our history lessons. Every student was able to study what fascinated them and apply it to the theme.

I had an older special-needs student who was obsessed with horses. Though she had Oppositional Defiant Disorder—which can include aggression and annoying others—as long as I linked her lessons to horses she cooperated. In this way, she made academic progress. I printed her math papers with horses on the edges. If we studied the middle ages, she and I explored the role horses played in those times. It was such a simple thing to fashion her lessons this way, and it motivated her.

The twins thrived in this environment. They imitated what they saw the older students do, and everyone was keen to interact with them. During recesses the twins had ample opportunities to practice appropriate social skills and develop language while playing with the other students.

Why recess for all the grades? For these students, a few who had been bullied so badly they could hardly hold up their heads, recess was just as important as class time. Some of them had either a special learning need or emotional disability. There were typical and gifted children in the mix as well, and these students were great role models. I believe that using large muscles throughout the day and being outdoors is something that is lacking in American education. God created children to move, not sit at a desk. We had three ample recesses every day.

In this little school my boys developed an imagination. Children with autism generally struggle with role-playing. But when one of my helpers learned the twins were obsessed with the Federal Bureau of Investigation, he encouraged them to act as if they were members of the FBI. He made them badges and gave them notebooks for taking notes. Many recesses were spent solving crimes and catching the bad guys (usually a high school student).

The Multilevel Classroom

I'm often asked how I managed to teach that many children and grades all at once. Here is how I fashioned our day.

8:30 AM—Arrive, Sharpen Pencils, Fill Water Bottles, Start Copywork

I allowed the students to keep a water bottle at their desk. This prevented them from interrupting lessons by asking for a drink. Also, in my years of working with children, I've learned that thirsty kids are inattentive kids who don't learn. I also allowed chewing gum for those students who were able to chew it. I never found gum on desks or chairs. Chewing gum is also a good brain organizer and helps students to concentrate.

Copywork was a morning ritual that included the children copying what I'd written on the board. Usually it was a Scripture passage or memory verse, but one year we copied all 110 of George Washington's *Rules of Civility* (one per day). Sometimes they'd copy a poem to put in their nature journals. Another year we copied inspiring Edgar Guest poems.

I modified the copywork for each student. Younger students used tracing pages or alphabet pages, depending on their grade level. I knew they were ready to start doing copywork from the board when they'd flip their papers over and copy on their own. The younger students wanted to be like the older students. This was a fabulous influence on the twins as well.

Why copywork? One reason is that it helped with visual and motor memory. The twins learned how sentences were spelled, spaced, and punctuated. As students progressed in English and language, they transferred these rules of grammar to their writing. It was also a way to immediately engage all the students before the bell rang.

Even the older students learned from copywork. We had notebooks dedicated to this and the older students had extra time to make their books beautiful keepsake items. I enjoy looking back at my sons' books and seeing how their penmanship improved. But I especially enjoy the drawings.

After I rang the old-fashioned school bell on my desk, we said our pledges to the American and Christian flags and the Bible. We recited a memory verse, books of the Bible, and other memory activities for the week, took prayer requests, sang songs (usually one patriotic and a few Bible songs), and had a short Bible study. The year we studied ancient history, I correlated the Bible studies with the history lessons. One year

we used Stick Figure Through the Bible. I highly recommend that curriculum. Each student draws stick figures on their level, from preschool
to high school. The older students were required to create more drawings
than the younger students, but in this way we were able to study through
the Bible together and engage everyone.

The twins remembered every single Bible story. In the beginning they
weren't able to repeat the stories back to me, but if I asked specific questions they answered them by pointing at illustrations. They were also con-
scientious prayer warriors and requested prayers for their pets every day.
It was exciting to see them grow spiritually. (See appendix A for more
information on how interventions were applied in our cottage school.)

We sat at tables as a class for opening exercises, Bible, and afternoon
classes. Younger students and students with more severe disabilities had
an adult volunteer sit next to them during group lessons. Wiggly children
were kept engaged with things for their hands to manipulate, such as
Legos or coloring pages.

9:00–9:45 AM—Math-U-See Curriculum

We did math first because it was the hardest subject for all my students to
grasp. I'd learned from teaching my own children at home that students
have the clearest minds before lunch. So, I hit the harder academics in the
morning. We split into age-appropriate groups for these hands-on lessons,
which used base-ten stacking blocks for every level, including algebra.
Most of the years Miss Mary worked with the preschoolers and the twins,
I worked with the elementary grades, and Miss Lois—one of the student's
grandparents—worked with the high school students.

9:45–10:15 AM—Snack and Recess

Snack time is especially important for special-needs kids. And what's
good for special-needs kids, I believe, is good for typical children. Snack
time wasn't only about the food. It was also an important time for communicating and socializing.

Students brought their own snacks and lunches, thus accommodating all diets. We encouraged high-protein snacks and veggies and fruit, but I admit sometimes a chocolate pudding made an appearance.

We mandated recess for all ages. We had a nice playground full of great equipment for climbing, sliding, and swinging. Students engaged sensory activities outdoors in full throttle. They also had room to play basketball and other ball games. I was fascinated by how much role-playing the students of every age engaged in. Being around such imaginative peers helped the twins learn to play too.

10:15 AM–Noon—English and Language

Kindergarten through third-grade students were given a reading program designed specifically for them. Some kindergarteners read on a third-grade level and some third graders read on a preschool level. Thankfully, I was familiar with several good programs. We used materials from Hooked on Phonics and A Beka Book (up to about third grade level), as well as *Tucker Signing Strategies for Reading*. Older students were provided award-winning books to read from the extensive library I'd developed over the years. I also checked out books from the local library.

Each day I listened to children read aloud and worked with them one-on-one. While I was working with students they also had language, phonics, and journaling activities. It wasn't easy at first, but they soon took pride in their work and their ability to work within the classroom rules.

Every child, no matter their age, did book reports. I allowed the students to choose their format, whether it was designing a marketing campaign, an oral presentation, or a video. This accommodated every child's learning style and abilities.

Every expectation and lesson in the classroom was as visual and tangible as possible. I kept a marble jar on my desk. If students completed their reading assignments, they put a marble in the jar. If they did homework (usually journaling and reading) or got 100 percent on a test, or if the class had an exceptionally good day behavior-wise, they put a marble in the jar. When the jar was full, we had a pizza party. This happened several times a year so that the reward time didn't drag on. Big marbles. Little jar.

Noon–1:00 PM—Lunch and Recess
Because we had special-needs students, lunch took longer than the average school's lunch period. And recess was extremely important for the students. During inclement weather recess was inside, but there was plenty of room to run and play. I'm happy to report that in the seven years we had the school, students didn't break a thing at the church facility.

1:00–1:45 PM—Teacher Read-Aloud Time
This was my favorite time of the day, and theirs too. I provided busy-hand activities, such as coloring, cutting and pasting, or Legos, and students of all ages came together to listen to stories or novels that usually correlated with our history theme. Older students sketched and were just as interested in this time as the other students. Children learned to sit quietly and pay attention. I'd stop during different points of the story and ask questions to ensure they were listening. I attribute their excellent habit of attention to the big-muscle activities they participated in during recess. (See my list of our favorite read-aloud books in appendix E.)

1:45–2:30 PM—Science/History/Art/Music
Because we wove our history lessons into our language lessons, we had history twice a week and science twice a week, and then we rotated extra days if we didn't have a field trip. School was over at two thirty. But before the final bell, since we didn't have a school janitor, we all pitched in with cleaning up. I assigned rotating chores and every student learned cleaning skills such as wiping down tables, washing the door windows, sweeping, vacuuming, straightening, cleaning the chalkboard, and putting away supplies.

Supplemental Activities

Field Trips
Our fabulous field trips were probably everyone's favorite part of our unique school. Each year we went camping for three days to learn more about how people lived without modern conveniences, such as electricity and running water. For five years we camped at a rustic campground in

tents. But on that fifth year it rained almost the entire time and I knew my tent-camping days were over. One year we rented individual cabins that were only big enough for four beds each. Another year we rented a large cabin on a nature preserve that had a large fireplace, basic kitchen, bathrooms, and two rooms on each end of the cabin with a dozen or so bunk beds. Boys slept on one end of the cabin and the girls slept on the other. I was still able to teach the concepts of "no electricity" by cooking outside, and there were many beautiful nature trails to study and enjoy.

Holidays

Each holiday, different age groups took part in creating a holiday meal. We celebrated them all. If it was on the calendar, there was a celebration. One year for St. Patrick's Day we had a green chocolate fountain and the children made lunch with all things green. These cooking classes resulted in one of our students graduating and becoming a chef!

But all kids love to cook, and the twins learned many things working in the kitchen that helped them with sensory issues and developed their academic thinking skills:

- Hygiene, such as washing hands
- Safety with equipment, such as knives
- Math skills, such as measuring, fractions, counting, reading numbers
- Science, such as observing, predicting
- Literacy skills, such as working left to right, letter and word recognition, prepositions, and new vocabulary
- Fine motor skills and eye-hand coordination such as kneading, stirring, pouring, and using utensils, including a spoon to measure out cookie dough

Sometimes we cooked things that we learned about in our history lessons or read-aloud book. This helped them learn about other cultures, but it also helped them to not fear trying new and unusual foods. To this day, the twins will try any new food, which is *not* easy for people with autism. They also learned independence and pride in creating something that other people enjoyed, and they learned to serve others.

The twins blossomed in our school's atmosphere because they were constantly engaged in meaningful activities. They learned to interact appropriately with other students with the guidance of parent volunteers. The patience of other students, and the gentle attention of Miss Mary, created an excellent learning experience for all the children.

Our school stressed manners, life skills, and appropriate behavior. Social skills were taught as much as anything else. Character was stressed, as was service to others.

Therapy

I was also able to access speech therapy for the twins through the public school, and one year we got a grant that enabled a special education teacher to come in several times a week to tutor the twins and other students one-on-one.

Lapbooking

Another way I kept so many different ages engaged in the same activity was through lapbooking. Homeschoolers are familiar with these wonderful activity books that children create themselves. Basically, they're academic scrapbooks made from file folders. Into these folders (refolded in unique ways) students pasted mini-projects, narratives, and research they amassed during a unit. For example, while learning about Old World explorers, students pasted such things as spices, gold doubloons made from foil, diagrams of sailing ships, and biographies of famous world explorers into their folders. We also pasted music, art, recipes, and lists of recreational activities from the same time period. (I've included a link in appendix E if you'd like to learn more.)

We worked on them together; the twins had a parent volunteer or Miss Mary sitting with them to assist. While we worked, we discussed the significance of each item, or I read information from an applicable book. Each child's folder was unique to their age level and ability. The more gifted students made elaborate folders. Everyone's individuality was celebrated.

Hands-on projects kept the students interacting with the material in a tangible way and made them more curious, thereby prompting as many questions from them as they received from me. It also kept their hands busy and was easy to apply in a multilevel classroom. No child was ever bored when we worked on lapbooks.

Physical Education

For physical education, we joined the community homeschoolers at the local college once a week for gym classes. College students in the adaptive physical education classes taught different age groups. This gave the students more interaction with other peers and helped the twins learn to cope with an unusual, unpredictable learning experience. There were tears the first few years, but by about the third year the twins were eager to participate.

On the last year we had the school, three students graduated from high school. It was a difficult decision, but the economy was bad and finances were strained. There were other factors indicating that it was time to make a transition in our lives. The Lord was stirring our nest again and urging me out of another comfort zone.

Chapter 14

Home for School

All your children will be taught by the LORD,
and great will be their peace.
—ISAIAH 54:13

The summer after the cottage school closed, I was excited to have the twins at home with me again. They'd made amazing progress in seven years, and I was eager to spend more one-on-one time with them now that our second son had graduated from high school. It was then that I signed a contract to write a book about Canada, and I debated whether to go back to school.

Working with the twins at home was very different than working with them when I had helpers like Miss Mary and Miss Dianna at the cottage school. However, I was blessed that Miss Dianna could keep them busy at church in the late afternoons so I could write and do my regular work. Afternoons with her were highly structured. She maintained the same routine and they always knew what would happen next. She kept them so busy they had no time to fuss at each other the way they did at home. I thanked God for her every day.

Twins can be demanding in terms of behavior in the first place. Couple that with teen hormones and autism and you've got a real exciting challenge.

To keep them from fighting or eating everything in the refrigerator, I had to be ever-present in their day-to-day schedule. They were growing into fine young men and I was very proud of their growth, but I was often concerned that I couldn't provide enough in terms of engagement and fresh learning experiences.

It wasn't easy keeping them meaningfully occupied. They wanted to watch TV all day. But that wasn't the sort of habit they needed to develop to become responsible young men. I had to re-evaluate my goals for them and what I wanted them to learn. Life skills were at the top of my list.

Homeschooling: How We Did It

I know there are families who homeschool in a way that doesn't include goals, and that's fine if that works for them and their children. I tend to be a list maker and planner. I'm very visual (I sometimes wonder if I have a little touch of autism myself); unless I see it in black and white, it's hard for me to remember where I'm going.

At the start of that school year I asked myself some questions about each boy. The things I wondered about looked a bit like a homeschooling individualized education plan:

- Social strengths?
- Educational strengths?
- Behavioral issues?
- Social interaction with parents?
- Social interaction with siblings?
- Social interaction at church?
- Social interaction in the community?
- Educational weaknesses?
- Goals for math this year?
- Goals for English this year?
- Goals for life skills this year?
- Goals for Bible class this year?
- Goals for social skills?

- Goals for language?
- Goals for community involvement?
- Concerns for the future?
- Goals for the end of this school year?
- Goals for the end of high school?

I always used a teacher's planning book for homeschooling. Sometimes I purchased one at the teacher's store and sometimes I made my own. I also used the free forms on Donna Young's Homeschool Resources website (DonnaYoung.org). If you have a printer and ink, you'll find every sort of form you'll ever need on that site. She also offers great homeschooling tips and guidance on how to plan. Usually my homeschool lesson plan looked something like the chart on the following pages (keep in mind this is a modified lesson plan for children with intellectual disabilities).

As you can see by my lesson plan, in the mornings we had Bible study, chores, and breakfast. This was followed by lessons in math and English. The afternoon was filled with life skills projects, and they spent most of their time with their dad before going to Miss Dianna's house for a few hours.

I don't mean to insinuate that we always followed my well-laid plans. When you live with autism, you live with the unexpected. That's why I dedicated a one-hour block to each individual subject. We by no means did math for an entire hour. Sometimes it took fifteen minutes to pick up a pencil, depending on their mood and temperament, not to mention life's regular interruptions.

Since my homeschooling philosophy leaned toward the Charlotte Mason method, I'd always understood the importance of keeping lessons short—especially in this day of technology. Kids' attention spans aren't very long. I used to think children could pay attention for about a minute per year of age. But now I wonder if it's not less than that.

Keeping lessons short was definitely the right thing for the twins, who tired easily when it came to pencil work. I always joked that they were allergic to pencils. But that wasn't the issue; it was simply hard for them

Week of	Bible 9:00–10:00	Math 10:00–11:00	Language 11:00–Noon	Life Skills 1:00–3:00	Afternoon
Monday	Prayer time John 1 Discuss	Subtract two-digit numbers without calculator	Articulation: "L" Journal Read library book; narrate back	Help Dad with floor in Sunday school room	Miss Dianna Cook supper Shower
Tuesday	Prayer time John 2 Discuss	Check yesterday's work with calculator	Write letter to Grandma Articulation: "R" Read library book; narrate back	Go on church visitation with Dad Speech therapy	Miss Dianna Make own lunch Shower
Wednesday	Prayer time John 3 Discuss	Subtract two-digit numbers without calculator	Journal Work on "wh" questions Read library book; narrate back	Help Dad and Mom get ready for Wed. night services at church Attend church tonight; help in children's classes	Miss Dianna Sort laundry Shower

Thursday	Prayer time John 4 Discuss	Check yesterday's work with calculator	Make birthday card for sister Work on "if" questions Read library book; narrate back	Help Dad with weeding around fence PE at college Mow	Miss Dianna Clean bathrooms Shower
Friday	Prayer time Watch *Jesus* movie Discuss movie	Help Mom estimate how much the groceries will cost this week	Write grocery list Go to library; interact with librarian	Grocery shopping with Mom	Miss Dianna Clean bedrooms Shower
Sat./Sun.	**Sat. Morning:** Clean bedrooms Do laundry Help with yard work **Sun. Morning:** Pick up doughnuts for church Go to Sunday school Attend morning worship services	**Sat. Afternoon:** Errands with parents **Sun. Afternoon:** Family dinner Rest	**Sat. Evening:** Prayer meeting at church Family dinner Lay out clothes for Sunday morning **Sun. Evening:** Church services	**Other:** Help Mom plan Sunday dinner	Shower

to form letters correctly. Their hands got tired rather quickly as well. They didn't have iPads or smartphones then or we would have used those in lieu of paperwork.

Even though lessons were short and we allowed for interruptions, we still kept to a routine. As a pastor's family, it wasn't easy. But they needed a consistent bedtime and wake-up time. Honoring their need for predictability and structure helped each day go a little more smoothly, emotions-wise.

Personal Hygiene

You may wonder why I included "shower" in a lesson plan. Showering continues to be a challenge to this day. If they aren't allergic to pencils, I'm almost certain they're allergic to water. They continue to be tactile-defensive. One trick I've learned is to buy them the strongest, most-pleasant smelling body wash I can find. It's amazing how dirty boys can take a shower and emerge still smelling like, er, dirty boys.

One of my friends has a son with Asperger's syndrome who still needs his mother to talk him through the shower; otherwise, he will stand there with the water running, not knowing what to do. He is highly intelligent but self-help skills continue to be a challenge. Children with autism need a lot of guidance for personal hygiene, and teaching these skills should be a part of any homeschool program. (See appendix D for a list of life skills to teach.)

Technology's Influence

I'm thankful I was able to teach my children before tablet and smart-phone technology became mainstream. I love technology, but I also loved curling up on the couch with my kids and a book. I loved spending time with the children in the woods and taking them to fascinating places. Now that they have iPads and iPhones, I don't get to snuggle as much. Okay, so they're also grown now. (Do you suppose that might have something to do with it?)

That's not to say you can't teach just as well, if not better, with technology. I'm convinced you can. Knowledge is readily at our fingertips now and I love my gadgets. I no longer have to haul sets of encyclopedias around. Nowadays I can put fifteen hundred books in my motorcycle saddlebag via my Kindle or iPad. I just wax nostalgic when it comes to papers, pencils, and books.

And yet, technology has helped the twins advance these last few years in remarkable ways, both socially and in personal life skills. They continue to surprise me with their ingenuity in finding unique ways to use it to communicate. Once, when we got a new washing machine, Isaiah was confused about which button to push. He took a picture of the settings with his phone and brought it to me to ask if it was right or not. It was, and he was tickled that he got it right.

They are also writing and communicating a lot more now via social media and texting. Keep in mind, they are twenty-two years old. I didn't allow them to use Facebook or text friends when they were younger. While I am still their guardian and oversee their posts and online accounts, having access to this media has expanded their language and social skills.

There are many excellent applications now for children with autism. I've listed a few in appendix E, but by the time this book goes to press, there will likely be many more. Nonverbal people with autism are communicating now because of iPad technology. Tablets engage children in ways we can't always understand, but I'm grateful because they've helped my boys' communication and social skills improve.

Schedules and Anxiety

By the time I was homeschooling the twins, I no longer needed picture schedules to help them through their day. The twins had progressed so well in reading that I could post their schedules in writing. And if I didn't, they'd get into my planner to see what I'd written down, which could be annoying. Whenever they saw something written on my calendar, they'd ask about it every five minutes until the date arrived.

Okay, maybe not every five minutes. More like every six. But if you have a child with autism, you know how they get very nervous about schedules and want to know exactly what's going to happen when. It's all a part of overcoming their fear of the unknown and their way of controlling any future scariness.

"Mom, why you write dentist May 15? We go or you go?"

"Mom, you write picnic June 14. It be too hot; we not go."

"Mom, it say meeting August 10. We go too?"

I have to remind myself when these conversations are going on that I waited a very long time to hear those voices. Once nonverbal, they're now so talkative some days that my ears hurt. Everyone in this family loves to talk. A lot. The twins fit right in.

I do try to keep a monthly erasable schedule on the hallway wall so the boys can anticipate a big change in their schedule, such as me taking time to edit a book or their father going overseas on a mission trip. But if it's something I know they are going to have a high level of anxiety about, I try to keep it to myself as long as I can, until they absolutely need to know about it. I keep appointments for such things as dentist visits and blood draws under wraps until a day or so before.

A Gentle Nudge

We continued to access speech therapy through the public school. It was through their speech therapist that I became familiar with a life skills program the high school offered for students with special needs. As a homeschool parent, I was wary of putting the boys in public school, for various reasons. But I wasn't convinced that homeschooling was the right choice for the twins as they transitioned into adulthood.

At around the same time, I read an article in the local paper about a high school special education teacher named Rhonda Bright. She'd led an effort to make a dying student's prom dreams come true. I was deeply touched; something inside me said, "You can trust someone with a heart like that."

A few weeks later I ran into this teacher at a rummage sale held at our church. Two high school students were raising funds to help with their prom expenses. I introduced myself and told her about the twins. She smiled and said, "I hope you'll give them the opportunity to come to the class."

Her words rang in my ears all summer and the next school year. After praying about it with my husband, we decided to give it a try. We could always pull them out and bring them home if it went badly.

I'm happy to report that giving the boys the opportunity to attend the high school life skills class was the best decision we could have made. They attended life skills in the morning for three hours and then took a bus to the vocational school in the afternoon. They completed two years in the carpentry program and received a certificate of completion. Because of their limitations, they weren't able to receive a certified high school diploma, but we are proud indeed of the certificate of completion they earned. The vocational school told me that they were two of the hardest working students they'd ever met.

Mrs. Bright is one of the kindest, most passionate, and hardest-working teachers I've ever known. I'm amazed at how God orchestrated the twins' lives and brought the right people into them at just the right time.

God is bigger than autism.

His timing is always perfect.

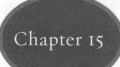

Chapter 15

Meaningfully Engaged in Community

Do you not know that in a race all the runners run,
but only one gets the prize? Run in such a way
as to get the prize.
—1 CORINTHIANS 9:24

The twins were three years old and I was in Walmart with them alone. Without a cart. In Bentonville, Arkansas. Walmart headquarters, USA. We lived just around the corner from the ultimate Walmart Supercenter, and I got the crazy idea that I could pop in, pick up some ibuprofen for a headache, and pop out. No problem.

Maybe it's my eternal optimism that made me forget how harrowing it is to take twins with autism into an oversize building that functions like a carnival on steroids. For whatever reason, I thought this was a good idea. And at first things went smoothly. I grabbed my ibuprofen in the pharmacy aisle and we headed toward the checkout.

But when we were walking past the toy section, Isaac spied a battery-operated jeep. The kind that kids get in and drive around. Even though he was nonverbal, Isaac made it abundantly clear that he was going nowhere until he commandeered that red vehicle and drove it straight home.

I managed to steer Isaiah past it, but Isaac wasn't having any of it. He laid himself down on the floor and proceeded to kick, flail, and scream. People stared at his red face and little balled-up fists and glared at me as if to say, "Shut him up or get him out of here!" I was sympathetic, but I knew if I tried to pick him up he'd go limp fish on me. There was nothing left to do but wait it out.

I pretended to leave and went an aisle away with Isaiah in tow. I peeked around the corner, but he didn't care that I was gone. He continued to scream as if he were being skinned alive. People walked past him and shot daggers my way. I shrugged them off and continued to spy on him from the safety of the vitamin section. I was certain that once he noticed I was gone he'd stop screaming.

But he called my bluff.

There's something about children with autism. They possess a sixth sense that's hard to explain. A *knowing* that we don't access. It's an intuitive ability that many women possess, but in my kids it's more pronounced. Isaac *knew* I stood nearby and he refused to relent.

It was one of those moments when seconds seemed like hours. I hid in the next aisle and watched him kick and scream for at least ten minutes. Finally, I decided customers had been tortured with his blood-curdling shrieks long enough. Somehow, we had to make it out to the van.

Had this been in the days of YouTube, someone would have recorded us and I'd have ended up on one of those scandal talk shows, depicted as a child-abusing mother. There was nothing I could do but take Isaac by the hand and try to get him out the front door. I'm embarrassed to admit I practically dragged him there. What else can you do when you've got a raging, flopping grizzly bear on one arm and a slippery escape artist the likes of Road Runner on the other?

We finally made it out the front door where a teen girls' club was holding a bake sale on the sidewalk. I was sweating, my arms shook with fatigue, and my head throbbed. Isaac escaped my grip, wrapped his arms around a cement pole next to the bake sale table, and screamed as if he'd been dropped in boiling oil. Every eye in that parking lot focused on me.

And all I could do was laugh.

And the more I laughed, the weaker I became.

I don't remember how long it took me to peel Isaac off that pole, but I must have, because here we are, nineteen years later, living in another state. It's been awhile since we've had any tantrums like that in Walmart, but experiencing peace in stores was hard-won and worth the price we paid to get there. It's what I call my desensitization theory.

Exposure not Enclosure

Because we took the twins everywhere we went, they were constantly exposed to situations that challenged their senses. It certainly wasn't easy. There were times when I didn't think it was worth it, and I couldn't have done it without help. But I knew from the books I'd read that they *needed* these experiences as much as they needed air to breathe. Painful? Yes. Worth it? Absolutely.

Too often, because parents can't access support, children are kept home in sensory-safe environments and never challenged to develop a tolerance for the uncomfortable. The more we exposed the twins to situations outside their comfort zone, the more they grew to tolerate them. Some of this exposure grew out of necessity—we had no choice but to take them along, especially to church, since their father is a pastor. But sometimes we exposed them to new situations on purpose. Our school field trips were one of many ways they grew to accept new experiences.

I have friends, a couple named Pedro and Ivette, whose son, PJ, has learned to go out in the community too. He's able to eat at restaurants with his parents and go for walks in the mall and to the park. His parents have worked with him, using his fascination with helium balloons and kites to help him learn to tolerate these situations. They have had such success with him that when there was a shooting threat at a mall, he evacuated with his parents without major problems.

The reason this impresses me is that PJ is extremely regimented and easily upset when there are changes in his routine. But if his parents hadn't worked with him through the years, would he have evacuated during the crisis? Children need to learn to obey and tolerate new situations for their own safety.

Like PJ's parents, I wanted to teach my children acceptable behavior. Once they learned to use pictures and signs to communicate, I taught them not to hit me, their father, or their siblings. I wanted them to contribute to society, not just exist in it. Discipline is difficult for children with autism because of their struggle to modulate their emotions. But I feel it's important to send messages of displeasure to them regarding violent behavior. I believe we do our children a disservice if we don't provide consistent structure and high expectations. If we raise our children without teaching them socially acceptable ways of responding to stress, we fail them. Once they are eighteen, the criminal system doesn't care much about autistic excuses and explanations.

Allowing children with autism to get by with things you'd never allow a typical child to do is a false form of grace. It isn't helpful. As parents, our choices in what we expect from them will influence the outcome. Of course, there are those children whose autistic symptoms are much more severe; only a parent can know how much their child can tolerate in terms of structure and discipline. What breaks my heart are scenarios I experience with higher-functioning children whose social skills aren't where they could be because autism has been used as an excuse for naughtiness. Spoiling a child, feeling sorry for them, or not expecting the best from them hurts them.

Parents can also learn a child's triggers and redirect them to help modulate their emotions. On PJ's blog (PedroJavier.org), beneath a picture of PJ writing in a notebook, his father, Pedro, writes:

> One of the tricks with living with children in the autistic spectrum is learning their triggers, since sometimes it takes very little effort to derail what could in 5 minutes turn into an epic meltdown. In our case, we learned over the years that if PJ is upset

and not listening to us, he will still read whatever I show him.
Those precious seconds that he has to spend reading whatever I
wrote serve as a speed bump and many times defuse the meltdown before it happens.

In this particular case PJ was upset because we had not planned
the outing as a shopping trip. I pulled out a notebook and started
writing things like "PJ is being too loud, PJ needs to lower his
voice," etc., and showed it to him. Once he had calmed down,
we asked him if he wanted to do a quick shopping run at Target
instead of the much larger shopping he had expected elsewhere.

In this photo, barely 5 minutes past the point we had pre-
dicted he would start screaming, he was calmly writing down his
shopping list.

Is there anything quite as magnificent as an involved, engaged, understanding father?

No, there isn't. The power of Dad cannot be underestimated. The twins'
father has had such a positive influence on them, I sometimes think he
was all they needed. (I know that isn't true, but his input into their lives
cannot be overstated.) As the mother of four sons, I am keenly aware that
only their daddy can teach them to be men, because I've never been one.

Single mothers desperately need positive male role models for their sons
with autism. My husband steps in as a role model at times for fatherless
boys. There is a huge need for Christian men to answer this call.

Special Olympics

Positive reinforcement works much better than negative consequences in
changing behavior. Catch your child being good and praise them. The
twins shine under a cloak of applause. People with autism are no different
than others in that regard. I know I can go weeks on one compliment.
Encouragement is a powerful motivator.

This is one reason that involving the twins in Special Olympics was
such a blessing. The adaptive physical education teacher at the local col-

lege, Dr. Kim Duchane, headed up the program and assigned college students to special athletes as coaches to prepare them for the games. Dr. Duchane also ran the homeschool physical education program and was very familiar with the twins. He always recruited excellent students to train the boys in track events.

Special Olympics gives children with intellectual disabilities a chance to shine. It also gives parents the opportunity to meet other families who have children with similar challenges. For me there's simply nothing more inspiring than these athletes' courage.

I was so impressed with the spirit of these games that I included an actual incident in my novel, *The Pastor's Wife Wears Biker Boots*. To this day, I think about how the entire stadium and those on the sidelines cheered one little athlete to the finish line during a fifty-meter dash. She ran with all her heart until she saw a girl sprint past her. She stopped and started to walk away. But a coach running beside her gently guided her back onto the track to finish the race. Everyone cheered and encouraged her to keep going.

A grin spread across the beautiful girl's face as she pumped her little arms and legs across the finish line. She was the last one to end the race, but she was met with open arms as the crowd roared with joy. For me, this delicate child's race symbolized the great race we all run under the gaze of a great cloud of witnesses as described in Hebrews 12:1: "Therefore, since we are surrounded by such a great cloud of witnesses, let us throw off everything that hinders and the sin that so easily entangles. And let us run with perseverance the race marked out for us."

This is an intriguing thought, isn't it? Not only do we have the Lord himself cheering us on and waiting for us at the finish line with open arms, but we have the encouragement of those who ran before us. Their godly examples inspire us to stay the course and reach our destination victorious.

Sometimes it's tempting to give up and get off track when we see others around us obtaining victory with less effort. Other parents' kids graduate from college, get driver's licenses, or make touchdowns at football games.

If we focus on their races instead of our own, we'll be discouraged and want to give up.

Just as we're to "throw off everything that hinders and the sin that so easily entangles" to run this race (not walk it), we need to remove hindrances from our child's race as well. In day-to-day life for children with autism, hindrances usually take the form of negative behaviors in public places. It's our job to help our kids run the race that God has marked for them. We must be diligent in helping them learn to navigate life well.

God has placed your child in a community, and they need your help to become a part of it. He's also placed them in a family: a living, breathing organism. It must be nurtured to remain healthy. In the next chapter, we'll look at some ways a family with autism can thrive.

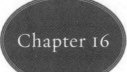

Chapter 16

Family Matters

God sets the lonely in families.
—PSALM 68:6

My favorite TV show growing up was *The Waltons*. I had a crush on John-Boy (a kindred spirit who loved books and writing) and was convinced that living on a mountain in a rambling farmhouse oozing with children was heaven on earth. I wanted to be like Mrs. Walton, who baked pies, made her kids' clothes, and was as calm as a cup of chamomile tea.

I blame her for my idealistic view of parenting. She made it look too easy. Before I knew it, my house oozed children, but homemade pies and hand-stitched clothes were nothing more than mirages in a desert of unfulfilled expectations. After the twins were born, I not only lacked time to sew but barely had time to shower and brush my teeth. Family dinners looked more like something from an indigent soup kitchen than the ones John-Boy's family enjoyed. Instead of smiling children politely passing the peas, mine were ducking to avoid plates of flying fish sticks and fries.

Family Strong

If I've given the impression in this book that my family has it all together, we don't. In fact, we're as dysfunctional as any family out there. Each day God's grace gets us through. If our family were to do a reality TV show—well, let's just say it wouldn't be pretty. Perfect we ain't. Marriage and parenting are the hardest work I've ever done. But there are some things I've learned that make a family strong.

Strong Families Set Boundaries

Children crave boundaries. A child without boundaries is an unhappy child. I can almost always identify a child in a crowd whose parents set no boundaries. They're usually the most surly and uncooperative. Your child with autism needs boundaries to be happy too.

Marriages also need boundaries. Besides essential parameters of faithfulness and purity, a marriage needs boundaries regarding the children. Parents must be united in their values and discipline. Each parent needs to know that the other parent supports them wholeheartedly. Children are smart and will use any small crack of disunity to divide and conquer. As David wrote: "How good and pleasant it is when God's people live together in unity!" (Ps. 133:1).

Strong Families Are Committed to One Another

Families who love one another lavishly and unconditionally—no matter what the circumstances—remain committed to one another. They set family goals together and remain united in reaching those goals. Openly loving one another, expressing appreciation for each other, and sharing important events together strengthens unity and commitment.

When children know that mom and dad and their siblings love them no matter what, they respond in kind. This creates a powerful bond. Overabundant, abounding love keeps a family strong. Unconditional love no matter the person's abilities, opinions, actions, or feelings creates a haven of safety and comfort. Differences are celebrated, not criticized. Scripture advises:

> Accept one another, then, just as Christ accepted you, in order to bring praise to God. (Rom. 15:7)

Above all, love each other deeply, because love covers over a multitude of sins. (1 Peter 4:8)

Strong Families Choose Their Words Carefully

Parents model for their children how to treat their siblings and other people in the world. Christian families should create a safe environment for discussing any subject openly, with truth and grace. Children who aren't afraid to express themselves will more likely come to parents when faced with difficult life choices. Absolute and unconditional love creates a safe place for children to openly share situations or questions that are troubling them.

When grace is modeled at home, children will understand God's mercy and be willing to go to him in times of need. "There is no fear in love. But perfect love drives out fear, because fear has to do with punishment. The one who fears is not made perfect in love" (1 John 4:18).

Shame, control, and intimidation have no place in the Christian home. Words have tremendous power, especially in the lives of impressionable children. Verbal or physical abuse should never be tolerated.

Unkind words from children should be corrected by saying something such as, "The Akins family doesn't speak to one another that way," or "The Akins family chooses kind words when speaking to one another." Remember, God created the world with words, and the power of life and death is in the tongue (Prov. 18:21). Children will become what you say they are. Your spouse will be built up or torn down by the words you use. "Therefore encourage one another and build each other up" (1 Thess. 5:11).

Strong Families Serve One Another

When each family member has responsibilities in the home, they feel like a valuable part. It gives children a sense of importance and belonging to have a role that other family members depend on. A child's self-worth is nurtured when they learn to be responsible. "For each one should carry their own load" (Gal. 6:5).

Strong Families Take Responsibility for Their Actions

Each family member is expected to face the consequences of their own actions and take responsibility for them. Wise, courageous parents allow natural consequences to teach their children. They do not rescue them from painful lessons. Instead, they allow God to instruct them through the cost. When parents make mistakes, they openly admit them and ask for forgiveness. This models for children the appropriate way to deal with shortcomings. It also comforts them to know that everyone makes mistakes and can learn from them. "For all have sinned and fall short of the glory of God" (Rom. 3:23).

Strong Families Forgive One Another

Parents who forgive one another teach their children to forgive others. Past offenses are not brought up and used against each other, and family members are given the opportunity to learn from their mistakes. Every day starts with a clean slate, allowing healing to occur. When someone apologizes, the response is always forgiveness. "Be kind and compassionate to one another, forgiving each other, just as in Christ God forgave you" (Eph. 4:32).

Strong Families Take Time to Celebrate and Play Together

Traditions are another glue that holds families together. Celebrating and playing together keep a family strong and build solid relationships. Passing down traditions gives family members a sense of permanence and importance. They can expect the same love and attention to be a part of their life in years to come. "I praise you for remembering me in everything and for holding to the traditions just as I passed them on to you" (1 Cor. 11:2).

Strong Families Have a Strong Foundation in God

Deuteronomy 6:4–7 teaches that the responsibility of instructing children about God is that of the parents. "Hear, O Israel: The LORD our God, the LORD is one. Love the LORD your God with all your heart and with all your soul and with all your strength. These commandments that

I give you today are to be on your hearts. Impress them on your children. Talk about them when you sit at home and when you walk along the road, when you lie down and when you get up."

Family Retreats

Because families must have positive quality time together to remain healthy, I'm a huge fan of Joni and Friends family retreats (see appendix E for details). Our family had the privilege of attending them twice. The first year, motorcyclists I met via an online forum called Women Who Ride raised money for our family to attend. The second year, our family received a scholarship. I can't stress enough how much I believe in this program. It brought much-needed relief and joy to us during two very stressful years. If you have a chance to go, by all means go. If you're looking for a charity to donate to, this one blesses many.

The retreats are held at different, handicapped-accessible conference centers around the United States. The entire family attends for a week in a safe, accepting camp atmosphere. Fellowshipping with other families facing similar situations was encouraging and helped me realize that others had a much harder race to run than I did. We participated in a wide range of activities, from boating to hiking to fishing. But my favorite part of the experience (besides the fabulous food) was meeting with other mothers and caregivers in daily group discussions. Evenings were spent in family-oriented activities, such as concerts, carnivals, square dances, and talent shows.

There were other details about the camp that made it extraordinary. When a family arrived, the entire camp staff lined up on each side of the hotel lobby entrance and applauded. It was like being on the red carpet. How many times do families living with disabilities get such an ovation?

We were also given a personalized welcome box prepared by volunteers at churches that included scrapbooks for storing camp memories, candles, DVDs, books, notebooks, body wash, and more. The welcome box had our name printed on it. We didn't feel like one of many. We felt individually loved and cared for.

I desperately needed the retreat the years we attended. I was absolutely devoid of emotion. I remember looking around at people enjoying themselves at the beginning of the week and wondering what it must be like to *feel* something. I was so burned out at that point in our journey that all I wanted to do was curl up in a dark corner alone and sleep forever.

Our rooms were beautiful, relaxing, and comfortable. Each family was assigned a short-term missionary (STM) per disabled family member. The STM was a volunteer—often someone who took vacation time from work to perform this selfless duty and assist the person with disabilities during their stay. This gave the parents and caregivers a much-needed break during all the activities, and the disabled person received direct support.

It was a week of freedom that I hadn't experienced in far too long. Personalized notes showed up at our doors each day with prayers, encouraging Scriptures, or poems. I've kept every little scrap from our family retreats in a special place in my office. Today, whenever I see that box, it makes me smile.

By the end of the week of that first retreat, joy was reawakened, not only in my heart but in my very bones. The light came back into my eyes and I was hungry to live life again. I made friendships that have stayed with me to this day. I grew stronger, more inspired, and grateful for the road God had me on.

Stress and Burnout

An often-overlooked consequence of autism is the effect it has on other members of the family. Besides parent burnout, it can also wreak emotional havoc on brothers and sisters. Because autism is unmercifully demanding, typical siblings can grow resentful and feel overlooked.

This is an issue I may have not paid close enough attention to while my children were growing up. If I had a chance to raise my children over again, I'd do a better job in giving my typical kids more one-on-one attention. I'd look for more opportunities for them to get a break from the constant pressures in our home. Because we are a forgiving family, I know my children will pardon my shortcomings, but I wouldn't be a human mommy if I didn't feel a little mother's guilt and wonder if I could have done a better job.

And, since I know I'm not alone in second-guessing myself as a parent, I hope you'll embrace a truth that God has planted in my heart: looking back wastes valuable energy that should be spent on going forward. I can't change any of my past mistakes, but I can move forward determined to be the best mother, grandmother, and wife I can be.

After all these years, my family is still intact. We aren't perfect, and we still have a lot to work on, but by the grace of God we are strong.

"Brothers and sisters, I do not consider myself yet to have taken hold of it. But one thing I do: Forgetting what is behind and straining toward what is ahead, I press on toward the goal to win the prize for which God has called me heavenward in Christ Jesus" (Phil. 3:13–14).

Chapter 17

The Importance of Prayer

Let us then approach God's throne of grace with
confidence, so that we may receive mercy and find grace to
help us in our time of need.
—HEBREWS 4:16

On the day we officially adopted the twins we held a party at the park after the court proceedings. We invited our friends to join us for a picnic, including every pastor in our small rural town (population six hundred). We wanted the ministers to pray over the boys; they were kind enough to take time from their busy schedules to lay hands on the twins' little heads and bless them.

I treasure that memory in my heart when I ponder God's beautifully orchestrated plan for their lives. Whenever we needed help with the twins, he sent it. Whenever they needed something, he provided. He continues to bless them far above and beyond what we could have ever imagined.

In those early days when they suffered from microcephaly, each time I changed the twins' diapers I prayed for their heads and spoke to their legs and told them that they would walk. "I'm not going to carry you all your life, so you will learn to walk, right?" Every. Single. Time. I spoke to those little bodies and commanded them, in Jesus's name, to grow and develop.

Miraculously, the boys' heads did grow. In fact, their heads are just right now for their nearly six-feet-tall frames. They also walk, run, swim, skate, ride bikes, and are extremely active young men.

I share this story not to imply that all children will walk if their mothers pray for them. That is simply not true. I don't understand God's ways because they are not our ways. But I do believe in going to him boldly for the things I need. Hebrews 4:16, which I opened the chapter with, teaches us that this is our right as Christians. Did I always remember to be so bold in my prayers? No. But I will always give him the glory for the many miracles he has given us these past twenty-two years. I can't wait to share some of them with you.

The Power of Prayer

Prayer is a mysterious thing. I'm eager to visit with God about it in heaven. Not that I don't ask him about it now. I'm a pest when it comes to asking questions about how and why he does things the way he does. But I get the feeling he doesn't mind my wanting to get to know him better. I want to know what tickles him, don't you? What delights God? What moves him? I want my Father to get a kick out of me. I want to give him a reason to dance.

Aren't you in awe that God himself hears us when we pray? That amazes me. When I think about how many voices are raised up to him in each moment of time, and that he still hears me and answers when I call, I feel much like King David when he wrote, "When I consider your heavens, the work of your fingers, the moon and the stars, which you have set in place, what is mankind that you are mindful of them, human beings that you care for them?" (Ps. 8:3–4).

If God is all-knowing, all-powerful, and all-wise, why does it matter if we pray? Can we change his mind? If he has a plan, will he change it?

What I do know is that he answers all our prayers. Sometimes he says, "Yes." Other times he says, "No" or, "Wait." Every time I've prayed according to his Word, I've gotten a positive response, or at least an alternative that made sense. I don't think I'm any more special than anyone else in that regard. God's Word works.

How Did Jesus Pray?
In the New Testament, Jesus taught his disciples how to pray. He told them to go into their own rooms and close the door and pray in secret. It's during this conversation in Matthew 6:9–13 that we read the words of what is now referred to as the Lord's Prayer:

> Our Father in heaven,
> hallowed be your name,
> your kingdom come,
> your will be done,
>   on earth as it is in heaven.
> Give us today our daily bread.
> And forgive us our debts,
>   as we also have forgiven our debtors.
> And lead us not into temptation,
>   but deliver us from the evil one.

When I'm overwrought or too tired to know how to intercede, and the words won't come, I pray the Lord's Prayer. Sometimes I end my daily prayer time with these words. I taught this prayer to my twins and we prayed it every morning at our cottage school. I'm grateful that Jesus gave us that beautiful supplication, along with the reminder to forgive others.

I take comfort in the fact that Jesus said our heavenly Father already knows what we need before we ask. Nothing we bring up to him is a surprise, but he still takes delight in our requests. When we ask him to meet our needs, we acknowledge that he is our provider and we need him.

And When You Pray, Forgive
An important aspect of our prayer life is forgiveness. In our walk with autism, we'll encounter countless hurts. People will disappoint us. Our expectations will be dashed and our hopes crushed. But we're still called to walk in forgiveness. One of my concerns as I grow older is that I become better, not bitter. I don't want to be a cantankerous old lady. I want to be

a sweet old granny who radiates wisdom and joy. The only way for me to end victoriously is to forgive those who hurt me. It's also a condition of God's mercy toward me.

Persistence

Another truth about prayer that Jesus taught is persistence. He taught this through a parable about a widow who wouldn't stop pestering a judge to answer her request. This judge had no conscience. He didn't care what people thought nor what God thought. And yet this little widow wouldn't stop believing that he'd answer her plea for justice.

At first the judge refused to listen to her case. But because the woman wouldn't leave him alone, he finally relented just to shut her up: "And the Lord said, 'Listen to what the unjust judge says. And will not God bring about justice for his chosen ones, who cry out to him day and night? Will he keep putting them off? I tell you, he will see that they get justice, and quickly. However, when the Son of Man comes, will he find faith on the earth?" (Luke 18:6–8).

A dear elderly lady once said to me during a lunch date, "I don't bother God with my problems. He has enough to worry about." I nearly choked on my sandwich. It never occurred to me not to bother God. I mean, he's *God*. He can handle it! And not only can he handle it, Jesus even taught us to pester him relentlessly.

And why not? God is persistent with us. He never leaves or forsakes us. He is always reaching out to us, longing for our friendship. And yet how often do we ignore him as if he isn't in the room? How would we feel if those we loved treated us the same way?

Another one of my favorite stories about petitioning God for others is the one about how Abraham boldly and courageously interceded for his nephew, Lot, after he learned God's intentions toward Sodom. Abraham asked God if he'd spare the city if there were fifty righteous people found within it. The Lord replied that for fifty righteous people he wouldn't destroy it.

But Abraham knew he might not find fifty righteous people. So, he appealed to God again. "What if there are only forty-five?" God in his mercy said he wouldn't destroy it if forty-five righteous souls were found living there.

But Abraham wasn't even sure forty-five righteous folks existed in Sodom, so he kept bargaining boldly with God until he got the number lowered even further: "Then [Abraham] said, 'May the Lord not be angry, but let me speak just once more. What if only ten can be found there?' He answered, 'For the sake of ten, I will not destroy it'" (Gen. 18:32).

God knew what Abraham was going to ask. He knew that Abraham would be persistent. And God honored that tenacity and boldness. Just because you don't feel that God is listening doesn't mean he isn't. You may not see an immediate answer, but that doesn't mean it's not on its way.

God's Word says, "He will respond to the prayer of the destitute; he will not despise their plea" (Ps. 102:17). He is not willing to turn a deaf ear to you. 1 John 5:14–15 says, "This is the confidence we have in approaching God: that if we ask anything according to his will, he hears us. And if we know that he hears us—whatever we ask—we know that we have what we asked of him."

However, prayer doesn't work like a microwave or a drive-through. Impatient Americans want immediate results, and if they don't see them, they get discouraged and give up. God's timetable isn't our timetable. What if God arrives with an answer and we've given up and aren't there?

Mighty Warriors

Praying is warfare. We can't begin to understand with our finite reasoning the invisible powers that go to war on our behalf when we call out to God:

> For though we live in the world, we do not wage war as the world does. The weapons we fight with are not the weapons of the world. On the contrary, they have divine power to demolish strongholds. We demolish arguments and every pretension that sets itself up against the knowledge of God, and we take captive every thought to make it obedient to Christ. (2 Cor. 10:3–5)

The enemy doesn't want us to pray because prayer moves God's hand. We know we need to pray because Jesus set the example for us. If Jesus, our Messiah prayed, what makes us think we don't need to?

Check Your Baggage

When we go to God with our burdens, we are no longer weighed down. We can give the yoke of autism to our Lord, and he'll carry it for us. We have this tremendous power at our disposal and yet sometimes, because we set our eyes on the autism instead of the Answer, we miss out on the blessings God has in store.

It reminds me of that story about a couple who went on a cruise and ate crackers in their room because they didn't know the bountiful meals on the ship were included in their fare. We've been given a feast of friendship from God that we fail to access when we do not pray: "Come to me, all you who are weary and burdened, and I will give you rest. Take my yoke upon you and learn from me, for I am gentle and humble in heart, and you will find rest for your souls. For my yoke is easy and my burden is light" (Matt. 11:28–30).

By depending on God and fellowshipping with him in prayer, our strength is renewed supernaturally. This is a power that one can definitely benefit from when raising children with autism. This supernatural strength isn't something that you can comprehend in the natural world. But I believe that God's Word is true, and I believe him when he says this in the book of Isaiah:

> Do you not know? Have you not heard? The LORD is the everlasting God, the Creator of the ends of the earth. He will not grow tired or weary, and his understanding no one can fathom. He gives strength to the weary and increases the power of the weak. Even youths grow tired and weary, and young men stumble and fall; but those who hope in the LORD will renew their strength. They will soar on wings like eagles; they will run and not grow weary, they will walk and not be faint. (40:28–31)

Those who hope in the Lord will renew their strength. A praying parent is a hopeful parent. Prayer allows us to soar like eagles.

I don't know about you, but when I'm in the trenches of an autism meltdown, I need an eagle's eye view. I need the ability to soar effortlessly through situations, not wear myself out flapping my wings in desperation. Prayer provides this kind of power.

Soaring is a peaceful, effortless experience. If you've never known what it's like to experience such peace, take time to pray. Talk to God as if he's standing in the room with you. He cares for you deeply and is so familiar with you that he knows the number of hairs on your head (Luke 12:7).

Now, I love my children, and I love my husband, but I don't know how many hairs they have on their heads. The fact that God knows this about me proves that he's really into me. He's concerned about what I'm going through and wants to share my burdens. And he cares not only about me but about everyone in my family the same way.

When our children hurt, we hurt. God is no different. His heart breaks when yours breaks. He longs to comfort and support you when you're in need. He's waiting to help you make this journey with your child. You don't have to do it alone. You have a Friend.

And he's only a prayer away.

Chapter 18

The Church's Call to Autism Ministry

Some men came, bringing to him a paralyzed man,
carried by four of them. Since they could not get him to
Jesus because of the crowd, they made an opening in the
roof above Jesus by digging through it and then lowered
the mat the man was lying on.

—MARK 2:3–4

When the twins were kept out of the Christmas program in 1998, it broke my heart. As I wrote in the introduction, when I discovered they weren't onstage, I left the sanctuary to find them hidden away in an empty classroom, banging their heads on the walls. The bewildered church janitor who'd been recruited to watch them breathed a sigh of relief as I stormed through the door, scooped them up, and took them home.

We didn't go back to church for two months.

This was a problem for several reasons. First, my husband was the youth pastor. Second, I knew it wasn't right to stay home and not attend church with my other children. Clearly, something had to be done.

169

That something came in the form of forgiveness and prayer. I wrestled tearfully with God, complained to him about their insensitivity, and ranted, "Why don't they do something? Can't they see it's not right that I can't go to church because they won't include my children? Don't they even care? How can they be so heartless?"

God never answers me the way I think he should. Does he answer you in strange ways too? It happened to Elijah when he fled from Jezebel to hide in a cave on Mount Horeb. He was complaining, wailing, and reminding God about all the good things he'd done when God said: "'Go out and stand on the mountain in the presence of the LORD, for the LORD is about to pass by.' Then a great and powerful wind tore the mountains apart and shattered the rocks before the LORD, but the LORD was not in the wind. After the wind there was an earthquake, but the LORD was not in the earthquake. After the earthquake came a fire, but the LORD was not in the fire. And after the fire came a gentle whisper" (1 Kings 19:11–12).

So there I was one Sunday, in the midst of a wind-earthquake-and-fire-weeping-and-wailing pity party, asking God why he didn't do something, when I heard a very small and gentle voice say, "Why don't *you* do something?"

I remember the exact moment. I was lying on my bed, staring at the ceiling.

I sniffed. What? Why don't *I* do something? Don't I have enough to do?

But as I considered it, ideas of how we could minister to families with special needs at our church poured like gentle rain into my heart. I knew we weren't the only ones with a desire to attend regular church services with other family members. I knew others, like me, didn't like being tucked away in a room somewhere, away from the rest of the congregation. There was an unmet need, a gaping hole that created a chasm between the church community and hurting families, and something was needed to fill it.

And so something did. After I forgave my church's ignorance, the idea of PALS—People Assisting Little Souls—came to life.

PALS

For Isaiah and Isaac to attend church successfully in the same classroom as their age-mates, they needed a person to shadow them. I decided to train people about autism so the twins could go to Sunday school and children's church like other kids. As I began to work on the details, I realized that such a program would benefit not only our sons but other families who felt their children needed the same assistance.

I approached the pastor and proposed the idea of a PALS program for all children with disabilities. Any parents who felt their child needed help to attend church could ask for a trained PALS volunteer. They would teach the volunteers about their child's disability and help the workers write a plan for successful church attendance.

In the plan, we included the child's unique strengths, needs, and any goals the parents had for their child's spiritual growth. For my children, I desired that they be included in all activities and that staff members be trained in understanding the culture of autism.

I got approval from the pastor to begin a PALS program, set up training sessions, and printed up PALS handbooks. The handbooks included a list of parent and caregiver advisors who could answer questions about working with exceptional children and adults. It also included job descriptions and expectations of PALS volunteers, tips on ministering to special-needs families, proper disability etiquette, and other helpful information.

During our first training, I chose to teach on the "culture of autism." The twins had been labeled by other parents and teachers in the church as naughty, spoiled, and out of control. I wanted to help people understand that the twins didn't live in the same sphere of reality as other children.

At our first training session, while people settled into their seats and looked over their notes, I turned up a radio's white noise. Another teacher flicked the lights on and off while I spoke to the class and made weird facial expressions. I pointed at them and tried to get them to follow my instructions to form a circle. That chaotic moment helped people understand what sensory overload could be like for children with autism.

I explained to the eager new volunteers that for very young children, the concept of God may be abstract. While they may not know who God is, they could still learn that church was a pleasant place to be where people were loved, accepted, and safe. Workers also learned about the fear and anxiety that are part of autism and the importance of familiarity.

Some people confuse including children with special needs in regular classes with "normalizing" them. They expect the exceptional child to conform to all the cultural norms of the classroom and act like their peers. But the goal of including the twins in regular church activities wasn't to change them, or train them, but to simply provide them the same worship opportunities as typical children.

This can be met with resistance from people who feel that all behaviors should be corrected. The fact that our sons tried to sniff the teacher's shoes when they sat in circle time was troubling to some. Prejudices can keep people from understanding that we don't all view and explore the world in the same way.

Human Nature

I'd like to tell you that once we implemented the program all went smoothly, but I can't. People are still people, no matter how many times they walk in and out of a church door. I got the message from some on the staff that if I'd just spank the twins they wouldn't have certain behaviors. But at that stage of their cognitive development, and in light of their severe sensory input issues, the only way to deal with most of their negative behaviors was to prevent them.

Some folks simply don't want to comprehend autism, and, frankly, I don't have the time or energy to waste to teach them. You won't win everyone over to the disability ministry way of thinking. That's okay. There are ministries that I don't have a burden for either. But we do need to respect other ministries, even if we don't understand them.

One of the things I desire for all Sunday school and children's ministry leaders to realize is that while young children with autism or the intellectually disabled may not be able to understand a Bible story, they can still learn a lot about God and love through multisensory activities. A flannel board character may not convey who baby Jesus is, but they'll love the soothing feeling of soft felt between their fingers. Moses parting the Red Sea can be demonstrated in water play. Manna in the dessert can be enjoyed as crackers and maple syrup. Church can be a happy time of pleasant sensations. Happy experiences occur when attentive, caring leaders use modifications to reach inside a child's autistic world.

In those days, Isaiah and Isaac were even more visual than they are now. They knew who drove every car in the massive parking lot, and it troubled them when someone wasn't parked in their regular space. When we drove by familiar people's houses, they knew which car was supposed to be in each driveway, and if it wasn't, it upset them. At the age of three, they memorized the routes to every place in town and didn't like to take different ways to familiar places, like church or the store.

Their extreme visual abilities were also their weaknesses. Instead of realizing the teacher was speaking to them, they'd focus on her buttons or her earrings. It was difficult for them to prioritize their environment so they could tune out what was irrelevant. Without visual cues, they were lost and became overwhelmed and disruptive.

Because children with autism are unable to empathize, the twins didn't understand that pulling hair hurt. They needed constant visual boundaries and visual cues to help them succeed in a classroom of typical children, and they needed a teacher who understood them. Thankfully, their teacher was willing to help us make accommodations and include PALS volunteers.

I scheduled PALS volunteers a month ahead of time and provided pictures of them to parents so they could talk to their children about them throughout the week. I let the twins hold their PALS photos so they could feel more in control when they met them on arrival to their class.

I also taught teachers and parents how to write social stories to prepare their children for changes in routines, such as special concerts or dinners. Change is terrifying for some children with autism, and at our church if they arrived expecting the same schedule and it didn't happen, this created over-the-top anxiety and often resulted in meltdowns.

Sometimes if we were running late and the classroom was filled with children, we took the twins to a transition room with their PALS volunteers before easing them into the main classroom. It was a quiet, dimly lit room with only a table and one or two toys. We also used this room if a child was feeling overwhelmed.

The best technique for keeping the boys from melting down at church was going for walks. I sometimes wonder how many pounds and inches their PALS volunteers lost while working with them. It seems they walked for miles. But it worked. I was able to attend church services with my age group, and so were they.

Here are some other things that worked:

- Taping their name tags to the floor and table to indicate where they were to sit each time
- Providing a squishy toy to hold to keep their hands from reaching for pretty girls' ponytails
- Using picture schedules
- Placing pictures on all the activity baskets to match their picture schedule
- Using a wait card for the teacher to give them to hold while waiting
- Allowing them to "hide" under the table during activity time as long as they weren't hurting anyone and were quiet

Ministry to the Whole Family

There are many more churches implementing special-needs ministries now than there were in 1998. These wonderful ministries also include support groups for families and siblings. If churches don't have these ministries, perhaps it's only because there aren't enough volunteers to implement them.

Our current church has about as many adults and children with disabilities as it does typical people. I can't imagine worshipping without them. People with disabilities have a right to attend church with their friends as much as anyone else does. It's my dream that all churches learn to accommodate this unreached people group. I've included links to such ministries, as well as several very good books, in appendix E.

One ministry that is sorely needed in the church is respite. This can be provided in many forms. Parents need to go on dates, and siblings need to have fun with their parents and each other. If churches can open their doors for an hour or two on a Friday night, it would give exhausted caregivers a chance to go grocery shopping, clean their homes, or have coffee with a friend. Some may even opt for taking a nap as they are often up several times during the night.

If a church can't find volunteers to provide respite, perhaps they can provide services such as shopping, cooking, house and garden maintenance, transportation to medical or therapy appointments, or taking the siblings out for ice cream. There is always something a person can do to minister to a family living with autism or other disabilities. They need only to open their eyes to see.

Hoosier PALS

When we moved to Indiana to our current church, we were welcomed by countless numbers of people who accepted the boys with open arms. In 1999, their PALS volunteer, Miss Dianna, dressed in an angel costume and walked the twins forward wearing shepherd costumes to worship the baby Jesus in their very first Christmas program.

I was never more proud of them in my life.

As they grew up, they had a PALS volunteer each Sunday to help them sit in "big church." Because I was (and am) the church pianist, and their father was the pastor, we weren't able to sit with them. Gradually the boys learned how to greet people during handshake time. Granted, they started by slugging people, but they don't do that anymore. Isaac loves to serve in church services by being an usher, and both are helpers in the children's ministry.

They've been in almost every Christmas program since their first one, and when they aren't onstage they are helping behind the scenes. There are so many ways they've learned to serve this loving, accepting congregation, including participating in the gift exchange night that is held the first Sunday night of every month. During this service, people have the opportunity to share a talent, read a poem, or share a testimony. It was during these events, in an atmosphere of unconditional acceptance, that the twins had opportunities to play music with their dad.

The boys have gone from being in great need of service to being young men who serve. God is no longer an abstract idea to them, but a very real friend. When they asked to be baptized, I knew that God had heard my desperate prayers so many years before. I wish you could meet them. If you're ever in Indiana and you see identical twin boys mowing a church lawn or serving a free meal at a community dinner, be sure to stop and say hello.

They're likely to shoot you a smile, offer you something to eat, and ask if there's anything they can do for you.

"I have no greater joy than to hear that my children are walking in the truth" (3 John 4).

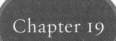

Chapter 19

Created to Serve

For we are God's handiwork, created in Christ Jesus to do
good works, which God prepared in advance for us to do.
—EPHESIANS 2:10

One year I directed a Christmas program at our church that included a cowboy choir, whose members used sign language while they sang. One of those cowboys was a nonverbal, elderly gentleman who loved to sing but had no words. He didn't have very many notes either, and his singing mainly consisted of loud, enthusiastic bellows. Every time he sang, I teared up at the sheer look of ecstasy on his face. The sounds he made with his voice were a passionate, joyful noise. As far as I was concerned, he was the best singer we had.

After the program, someone commented to me that most churches wouldn't have allowed him to sing in the choir because his sounds "ruined the music." While I agreed the harmony wasn't something we earthlings would consider technically excellent, I believed that heaven enjoyed it just as well, if not more. This man loved to sing and he used his voice to praise the Lord with all his heart. He was serving the Lord with a voice that seemed horribly imperfect to us, but I doubt it was imperfect in the eyes of God.

Purpose and Ability

Just because someone has a disability doesn't mean they don't have a purpose. God doesn't make mistakes and his Word applies to everyone, disabled or not. God has a job for each of us to do. For those who can't easily recognize the part they play in the body of Christ, it's up to others to provide opportunities and guide them.

The twins have been given more opportunities than most because they're pastor's kids. They've accompanied their dad and me everywhere and helped us with every imaginable responsibility in the church. From visiting the sick in the hospital to setting up tables for a dinner, they've learned to serve others with their gifts. This service carries over in their day-to-day lives as well. They have willing, helpful hearts.

Their father has kept them busy through the years laying floors at the church and doing drywalling and other carpentry-type work or maintenance. How blessed they are to have a dad who loves to spend time with his children. Everywhere their pastor-dad goes, they go. My children know more people in the community than I do. And most people don't know they have a diagnosis of autism until they are around them for longer than a few minutes.

If someone's arms are full, they offer to help them carry something. If they see someone struggling with a door, they hold it open. Of all the things they've learned, these are the skills I most admire. Because they were given opportunities to serve at very young ages, they've grown to help others. And not only do they help others when asked, they recognize when others need help. This is a huge accomplishment for any young man, let alone one with autism. I'm amazed that they're capable of doing such things, since two of the social skills people with autism struggle with are empathy and initiation.

I don't think their servants' hearts are completely a natural ability. Call me a fanatic, but I have a deep belief that God's hand is on their lives. I believe they hear his voice. Here's why: the twins often tell me that God speaks to them.

Who am I to say he doesn't?

Just the other day, Isaac came home all excited to tell me something that happened while he was running an errand for me.

"Mom, I was on way home. God tell me Miss Judy need help. I turn bike around, go back, and help Miss Judy."

"Miss Judy? Your Sunday school teacher?"

He nodded. "Yeah. She need help. God told me that."

"What did she need help with?"

"Boxes too heavy. She need help with boxes at storage. I move them. That nice; right, Mom?"

I smiled. "That's very nice, Isaac. Miss Judy shouldn't lift heavy things."

Isaac laughed. "God tell me that! God talk to me. I turn bike around and do what God say. I hear him say it."

"That's awesome, Isaac. It's important to obey God's voice when you hear it."

"Yep."

Now, I'm not saying the boys are always giddy with excitement when it comes to doing the dishes or cleaning the toilet. They're normal young men. But doesn't that make the fact that they love to serve others even more remarkable? I think so.

My hope is that all parents would help their children with or without disabilities to learn to serve. It's for service that God created us, as affirmed by this chapter's opening Scripture, Ephesians 2:10.

There are no distinctions in this verse regarding ability. Every person is God's sacred handiwork. We all have assignments from God. These tasks aren't always jobs or chores within the walls of the church. They include giving people with disabilities opportunities to serve in ministry, which helps them carry that serving attitude over into their day-to-day lives. It helps them discover talents they may not otherwise know they have.

It also gives them a sense of purpose. We all possess a need to contribute. I can't imagine going through life wondering why I was created. That has to be a desperate feeling. When we help others to believe in their purpose, we give them a reason for living.

I'm not sure if giving the twins opportunities to serve helped them develop empathy or not, but it's an interesting theory. They've gone from not understanding how other people feel when they hurt to having extreme compassion for the elderly and infirm.

Their paternal grandmother has Alzheimer's and lives with us. I didn't realize how much they cared for her well-being until the day she fell on our cement driveway, hit her head, and was knocked unconscious. The twins' extreme reaction of despair and panic was eye-opening. People who have no empathy wouldn't react that way.

Watching them gently care for her each day pricks my heart. They offer her food and make sure she drinks her protein shakes. Isaiah opens the bottle for her and says, "Drink it all gone, Grandma, so you get big muscles." Then he squeezes her bicep. These boys have come a long way from the days they refused to role-play with dolls and stuffed animals. Now they care for God's people and creatures with such tenderness that my heart explodes watching them.

The Church's Response to Autism and Disabilities

There are many opportunities for ministry in the church for young people with autism, but sometimes ministry leaders need to be made aware of them. Here are a few you might consider discussing with your church:

- Greeting (a great way to practice handshakes and eye contact)
- Opening/holding doors
- Folding bulletins
- Stuffing envelopes
- Making copies for teachers/musicians
- Making coffee
- Stocking pop machines/vending machines
- Mowing
- Sweeping/vacuuming/dusting/cleaning bathrooms
- Passing out or helping prepare refreshments for children's ministry
- Ushering in midweek services or small Bible studies
- Clearing tables at community suppers

- Passing out napkins
- Helping set tables for dinners
- Passing out bulletins/announcements
- Decorating bulletin boards
- Organizing shelves
- Helping with landscaping/flower gardens
- Taking out the garbage
- Doing dishes in church kitchen
- Collecting kitchen linens for laundering
- Making get-well cards
- Passing get-well cards around church to be signed
- Passing sign-up sheets for dinners/activities
- Helping put equipment away
- Running a DVD player for children's ministry
- Organizing DVDs for children's ministry
- Helping children with take-home bags
- Helping fill treat bags on holidays
- Wiping down tables
- Putting away extra chairs/tables
- Helping decorate for holidays
- Helping hang Christmas lights
- De-icing sidewalks
- Shoveling snow
- Walking elderly folks to and from cars
- Helping with fund-raisers, such as garage sales or food booths
- Helping visiting missionaries set up and tear down exhibit tables
- Helping visiting ministries by showing them facilities or setting up tables
- Helping with lighting/visual aids/sound

There are countless ways people with disabilities can serve in their local churches. They need only to be given the chance. Just as God gives us, with all our frailties and limitations, an opportunity to serve him, the church must allow those with disabilities to contribute as well. Compared to God's perfection and power, how feeble we are! But our Father doesn't see us in terms of what we *can't* do; he sees us in terms of our potential.

It's the church's responsibility to "speak up for those who cannot speak for themselves, for the rights of all who are destitute" (Prov. 31:8). If the church doesn't answer the call, how can we expect the world not to discriminate? As Christ gently guides us toward our calling, the body of Christ should embrace those with autism and show them how very valuable their contributions are.

Created for a Purpose

God makes it clear in the Scriptures that he has a purpose for each life:

> Listen to me, you islands; hear this, you distant nations: Before I was born the LORD called me; from my mother's womb he has spoken my name. (Isa. 49:1)

> The eye cannot say to the hand, "I don't need you!" And the head cannot say to the feet, "I don't need you!" On the contrary, those parts of the body that seem to be weaker are indispensable. (1 Cor. 12:21–22)

It hurts the body of Christ when one of its members isn't allowed to serve because it causes the body to be weaker than it should be. If there was ever a time when all of the body's members needed to be a part, it's now. We need those with autism to serve because we learn valuable lessons from them, and they strengthen us as a whole.

We mustn't enable anyone with autism to hide their talents and resist serving out of fear. On the contrary, we must do all we can to allow them to experience the words every Christian servant longs to hear from their master's lips: "Well done, good and faithful servant! You have been faithful with a few things; I will put you in charge of many things. Come and share your master's happiness!" (Matt. 25:21).

Chapter 20

Pie in the Sky

With men this is impossible, but with God
all things are possible.
—MATTHEW 19:26 (NKJV)

The developmental psychologist sitting beside me at her desk watched my four-year-old boys flip her office light switch on and off and pull one another's hair.

"What are your hopes for your sons, Mrs. Akins?" She turned to her desk and flipped open a notebook.

I took a deep breath. "I want them to learn to read, get jobs, live independently, and be contributing members of society."

She paused, threw down her pen, and clicked her tongue. Swiveling her chair to the side, she leaned forward and rolled her eyes. "Look. That's just pie-in-the-sky thinking, and you might as well give it up now. Their limitations are far too profound. You need to accept them as they are."

I don't remember what she said next. We walked out and never returned.

We may have made a few wrong decisions raising the twins, but that wasn't one of them. I refused to surround them with negativity when they were little. If one professional couldn't be positive about their futures, I found someone who could.

All Grown Up

When God brought us to Indiana, I had no way of knowing that these little boys would grow into the incredible young men they are today. I know we have a lot of learning ahead of us. I've never parented adult sons with autism before and I'm sailing through unchartered waters. We have some challenging seas yet to navigate: dating, adult friendships, and possibly living alone one day. But I don't fear the future because God has brought us this far and he will be faithful to steer us safely the rest of the way.

We continue to work on challenging behaviors. Identical twins are extremely bonded but they also annoy one another. Every day one of them is determined to move out of the basement they share and take up residence elsewhere so he can live by himself.

It's yet to happen.

I know we have girlfriend/boyfriend issues to face as well. One night Isaiah informed me that a girl in town—one with special needs—had crawled in through the basement window to visit Isaac. She was much older than Isaac, and it terrified me. No one has managed to slither into the basement since, but I'm not naive enough to think something similar couldn't happen again.

One of the most enjoyable things we experience with the boys is taking them to funny movies. It's more fun watching the twins laugh than seeing the movie itself. Their giggles are contagious and they get extremely involved with the antics on the screen. I can never get enough.

Do you suppose God enjoys watching us laugh too? Do you think he wants to take pictures when we make silly mistakes? I wonder if he and Jesus elbow one another, slap their knees, and laugh at our playfulness. I like to think that maybe they do.

I've learned so much about God by parenting the twins. His loving nature has been revealed to me in an incredible, intimate way. My love for my adopted sons is deep and unconditional. His love for me is the same. My acceptance of them, just as they are, reassures me that God loves me even more: "See what great love the Father has lavished on us, that we should be called children of God! And that is what we are!" (1 John 3:1).

The boys are hard workers and it's to their credit that they've come as far as they have. By God's grace we came across the right information at the right time to help them learn. By his grace, he placed loving people in their lives who focused on their abilities rather than on their limitations.

I know his grace will carry us through the challenges of adulthood, but I admit that sometimes I feel afraid. There are too few supports out there, and the prospect of a group home is terrifying. There is a shortage of programs for adults on the autism spectrum. Society hasn't kept up with the growing demand as autism rates rise and children grow into adulthood.

I refuse to worry, though. The same God who began this good work in the boys will be faithful to complete it for the rest of their lives. Do I fret a little about what may happen to them after I die? Of course. I'm their mother. Yet deep down I have the assurance that he will provide and care for them even better than I can imagine, just as he did when they wrecked Miss Jo's van.

Mountaintop Tumble

Never underestimate the keen observation of a three-year-old boy with autism. These nonverbal little guys knew much more than they could tell us, and we often found out the hard way. That's how Miss Jo's van ended up on the side of an Ozark mountain.

One Saturday morning, as we were wont to do, Miss Jo and I strapped the boys into their car seats and went garage sale hopping. This was a favorite hobby of hers, and it kept the boys from fussing for a while before lunch and nap time.

After we'd driven around for a bit in scenic Bella Vista, Arkansas, we made a run back home so I could use the bathroom. When I went into the house, Miss Jo decided that she'd pop into the front hall bathroom, just a few feet away. She opened all the doors on the van and flew into the house. I don't think I was in the house more than three minutes, and when I stepped outside my front door, the van was gone.

You know those cartoons where the character's feet are moving but they aren't going anywhere? That's how I felt as I screamed and ran in the direction the van had been facing, toward the end of the cul-de-sac. As I got to the street's edge where it dropped off into a small canyon, I could see the tail end of the van sticking up. In the back window were two terrified little boys banging on the glass, screaming and signing, "Mama" and "Help."

I don't remember how we extracted them from the van, but I do remember the thin baby tree that stopped it from careening to the bottom of the rocky ravine. We had no idea the twins knew how to get out of their car seats, and we certainly didn't know they could turn on the ignition and put a vehicle into drive. From that moment on I never underestimated them. I knew that inside those little earthly bodies were capable, gifted souls.

We called a tow truck, but the van was a total loss. Miss Jo could have lost her cool, but she didn't. I'm grateful to this day that we held the boys, praised God together that they were safe, and later, when the shock was over, laughed. I will never forget their little faces in that window and their cries for Mama. And I will never forget how God's protective hand kept them from harm.

Are there special angels for children with disabilities? It sure seems that way. Even better, there is a loving Father who knows everything they need and who is always present with them. I find great comfort in that knowledge. The world is filled with evil forces that influence people to be cruel. It's a lifelong challenge to teach the boys how to recognize when they're being taken advantage of. I long for them to have friendships that bless them as much as they bless others.

If my husband and I experience any success as parents, the power comes from God, not us. Certainly, there are seasons in this autism walk that are difficult, but we survive. In the early years when the boys screamed nonstop, it was easy to get discouraged. Even so, God never abandoned us. When we feel struck down and criticized for choices we make, we're not destroyed. "We have this treasure in jars of clay to show that this all-surpassing power is from God and not from us. We are hard pressed on every side, but not crushed; perplexed, but not in despair; persecuted, but not abandoned; struck down, but not destroyed" (2 Cor. 4:7–9).

You Gotta Laugh

All in all, living with these guys is a blast. Funny things happen that we don't expect, and we never know what might happen next. The boys have a great sense of humor and the ability to laugh at themselves when they make silly mistakes.

A few years ago, on Thanksgiving, I was out of canned pineapple. I needed it to make the twins' favorite salad, so I sent Isaiah to the store for "two large cans of pineapple chunks." Keep in mind that people with autism are extremely literal. You can probably guess what he brought home. Isaiah stumbled through the front door proudly bearing two heavy, gallon-sized cans of pineapple. We all laughed and took pictures of the purchase for posterity's sake.

"Mama, you say large pineapple, I get large pineapple."

"Yes, you did, Isaiah. You did exactly what I said."

Just a few weeks ago, when I was working at the church office, my husband texted me a picture of my kitchen counters covered in bananas.

"What is that?" I texted.

My husband wrote back, "I sent Isaac to the store for nine bananas. He came home with nine bunches."

So they make mistakes because we aren't clear enough in our requests. But they are going to the store *alone*, riding in a golf cart they drive *themselves*, and reading road signs *independently*.

How's that for pie in the sky?

Ultimate Destiny

Because I'm a follower of Jesus Christ, I believe the twins' ultimate destiny is a home not on earth but in heaven above. A person can have a doctorate degree from the most prestigious university on earth and still flunk heaven. It's not how smart or clever anyone is that matters in the end. What matters most, I think, is how much did we love?

Autism isn't forever, but love is.

When a teacher of the law asked Jesus which commandment was the greatest, he answered: "'Love the Lord your God with all your heart and with all your soul and with all your mind and with all your strength.' The second is this: 'Love your neighbor as yourself.' There is no commandment greater than these" (Mark 12:30–31).

There is great love in this house and community because the twins are in it. Oh, there are great challenges too, but at the end of the day it's love that prevails. It makes our rocky paths smooth and pours the oil of gladness on our wounded souls. There is a compelling, eternal light inside my boys. This autism gig isn't permanent. There are infinite, everlasting things in store for those who believe: "Therefore we do not lose heart. Though outwardly we are wasting away, yet inwardly we are being renewed day by day. For our light and momentary troubles are achieving for us an eternal glory that far outweighs them all. So we fix our eyes not on what is seen, but on what is unseen, since what is seen is temporary, but what is unseen is eternal" (2 Cor. 4:16–18).

It's the power of God that lives inside my children. He is the one who enables and inspires my boys and me. My prayer for you is the same as Paul's for the Ephesians:

> I pray that out of his glorious riches he may strengthen you with power through his Spirit in your inner being, so that Christ may dwell in your hearts through faith. And I pray that you, being rooted and established in love, may have power, together with all the Lord's holy people, to grasp how wide and long and high and deep is the love of Christ, and to know this love that surpasses knowledge—that you may be filled to the measure of all the fullness of God.
>
> Now to him who is able to do immeasurably more than all we ask or imagine, according to his power that is at work within us, to him be glory in the church and in Christ Jesus throughout all generations, for ever and ever! Amen. (Eph. 3:16–21)

Appendix A
Occupational Therapy and Teaching Strategies

H ere are only some of the ways a few helpful interventions were integrated at home and at our cottage school. To list them all, I'd have to write another book!

OCCUPATIONAL THERAPY-TYPE ACTIVITIES

Activity	At cottage school	At home
Calming	Deep pressure back rubs	Deep pressure back rubs
	Blankets	Weighted blankets
	Weighted vest	Weighted vest
	Beanbag chair	Beanbag chair
	Quiet, soft chair in quiet room under table	Parent holding and rocking
Vestibular activities	Blanket fort	Blanket fort
	Mini trampoline	Mini trampoline
	Allowing tasks/ assignments to be done while lying on stomach; also during read-aloud story time	Understanding that trunk strength is weak, allowing time on the floor

Activity	At cottage school	At home
Vestibular activities (*cont.*)	Swinging on the playground	Time at the park swinging
	Recess time to run	Outdoor time
	Trips to forests, nature preserves	Fishing, hunting for frogs in pond
Proprioceptive activities	Helping carry heavy items, such as boxes of books, chairs, or supplies	Helping with chores, such as mopping, carrying laundry, or yard work
	Playing with play dough	Playing with play dough
	Large pillows for punching	Pillows for punching, punching bags, oversized boxing gloves to box with siblings
	Playing tug-of-war with peers	Playing tug-of-war with dogs
	Exercising between subjects, such as stretches or knee bends	Doing chores
	Wheelbarrow races with peers	Wrestling with brothers
	Vacuuming classroom	Sweeping kitchen floor
Tactile defensiveness	Finger painting	Playing with pudding or shaving cream
	Play dough	Play dough
	Making cookies and decorating them; making pies; making bread; other cooking activities	Decorating Christmas cookies; cooking activities
	Crafts	Crafts
	Lapbook creations	Scrapbooking
	Nature studies—handling bugs, frogs	Catching frogs from the pond; fishing
	Allowing pets to visit	Playing with family pets
	Handwriting Without Tears curriculum	Tracing in sand, rice, shaving cream

Activity	At cottage school	At home
	Spelling words in trays of rice	Handling carpentry items such as nails
	Wearing costumes for school plays	Wearing costumes for church Christmas programs
	Papier-mache	Wrapping Christmas gifts
	Art projects that have texture	Allowing access to craft supplies
	Cooking	Cooking
	Working with glitter	Using sprinkles to decorate cookies, cakes, ice cream
	Hugs	Hugs
Tactile discrimination	Handwriting Without Tears curriculum	Puzzles
	Making puppets	Lacing projects
	Collages with noodles, cereal, rice, beans, etc., or nature items such as tree bark, sand, rocks, leaves	Glue-line collages/pictures. When glue dries, color between the glue lines by feeling
	Playing games with dominoes—touching and feeling the dots while playing	Playing "chicken foot" at church game nights (uses dominoes)
	Using Scrabble pieces to practice spelling words	Playing Scrabble
	Learning to touch type on computer	Learning to touch type on computer
	Drawing spelling words on back	Drawing on back
	Sewing projects, such as making pillows, latch-hooking, or cross-stitching	Folding clothes and talking about the textures while running hand over fabric
	Manipulating felt letters and numbers on felt board	Playing with felt characters on felt board

Activity	At cottage school	At home
Bilateral integration (midline crossing activities)	Placing school supplies where child must cross arm past midline of body to retrieve them	Setting the table for dinner
	Clapping while singing	Clapping while singing songs in church or Sunday school
	Writing/drawing on chalkboard without turning body	Sidewalk chalk art
	Passing papers down the row	Passing food at the table during meals
	Crisscrossing arms during class prayer	Crisscrossing arms during meal prayer
	Stretching; touching toes with opposite hand	Pilates with video
	Rolling out cookie dough	Rolling out pie dough
	Using scissors for lapbooking, crafts	Using scissors for crafts
	Assigning erasing chalkboard as a chore	Washing windows
Motor planning	Playing follow the leader	Playing follow the leader
	Acting out history and science lessons	Acting out Bible lessons
	Playing charades	Playing charades
	Using sign language or motions to songs	Using sign language or motions to songs at church
Fine motor	Using scissors, pencils, glue sticks, paint brushes, kitchen tools/utensils	Allowing use of scissors, glue sticks, pencils, paint brushes, forks, knives, spoons, spatulas, etc.
	Handwriting Without Tears curriculum	Writing/making cards for family members

HOW WE DID IT AT THE LCA COTTAGE SCHOOL: 2ND–8TH GRADES

Skill	Components of cottage school experience that helped skill to develop	Components of family life experience that helped skill to develop
Waiting	Sharing glue, colored pencils, and other supplies during lapbook making	Waiting for family prayer of thanks before eating
	Listening to others during prayer request time and waiting turn to share	Waiting for all family members to be in seat belts before parent starts the car
	Waiting at the door for the teacher to take class to the playground	Waiting to eat drive-through fast food until arriving at home
	Waiting for other students to come to snack/lunch table before giving thanks for food	Waiting until all family members are present before starting a movie
	Waiting to eat until after giving thanks for food	Waiting for pizza to be delivered
	Waiting to unwrap gifts at Christmas	Waiting to unwrap gifts at Christmas
		Waiting for friends to arrive for a visit
Taking turns	Playing chess	Playing UNO
	Pocket chore chart that rotates chores between students each day	Pocket chore chart that rotates between family members each day
Engaging in imaginative role play	Playing FBI and other imaginative role-playing games at recess	Pretending to work on bikes
	Taking part in Christmas programs and other school plays	Pretending to be carpenters while "helping" Dad with remodeling jobs
	Acting out Bible stories	Playing parts in Christmas programs

Skill	Components of cottage school experience that helped skill to develop	Components of family life experience that helped skill to develop
Greeting others	Visiting the library	Attending church each Sunday and Wednesday
	Greeting teachers and peers at school as they arrive	Accompanying parents on hospital and home visits to parishioners
		Accompanying parents on errands
Initiating	Visual schedules that inform student what comes next	Access to toys and art supplies within reasonable parameters
	Asking leading questions during play times: "Would you like to play with the red car or the blue car?"	Pictures of choices of things to do
	Praising and reinforcing all initiatives	Pictures of chores and routines
	Access to art supplies during free time	Access to toys and objects that fascinate the student
	Access to objects that fascinate and engage the student	Cooking/preparing own breakfast
Being flexible	Field trips and outings	Attending Sunday school, church, and midweek church services with support
	Camping trips	Going on errands with parents
	Unexpected changes in routine, such as not being able to go outside due to weather	
Being quiet	Bible time	Attending Sunday school, church, and midweek church services with support
	Story time	

Skill	Components of cottage school experience that helped skill to develop	Components of family life experience that helped skill to develop
	Visiting the library	
Modulating emotions	Deep pressure rubs by teacher	Deep pressure rubs by family members
	Hand signals from teachers to indicate when child is overexcited to prompt them to calm down	Sign language from parents to indicate when child needs to calm down
	Quiet room/area with soft chair	Quiet area in the home where child can calm down
	Many opportunities in which to practice range of emotions, such as field trips	Many unexpected opportunities to practice modulating emotions, such as running errands with parents and church attendance
	Using emotion charts to help child understand and express emotional state	Using emotion charts to help child understand and express emotional state
Finishing tasks (knowing when something is finished/when to move to next activity)	"Mailing" finished work to teacher using an actual mail box on teacher's desk	Taking dishes to the sink after meals
	Having organized, structured learning space where everything has a place	Organize home, where everything has a specific place
	Visual schedules for each activity, calendars, or moveable pieces of schedules to remove when task is finished	Visuals, such as calendars, chore charts, schedules for Saturdays; child removes item from schedule after activity is complete
	Softly ringing bell between activities or allowing child to ring the bell; using timers	Timers

Skill	Components of cottage school experience that helped skill to develop	Components of family life experience that helped skill to develop
Transitioning between activities without meltdowns	Routines—following schedules as much as possible	Routines—doing things in the same order throughout the day as much as possible
	Giving 10-minute, 5-minute, 3-minute, 2-minute warnings before new activity	Giving 10-minute, 5-minute, 3-minute, 2-minute warnings before new activity
	Providing adult emotional support	Talking through each transition
	Using transition objects—something to hold in hand to signal next activity, such as a favorite toy for story time or math blocks for math time	Using transition objects—something to hold in hand to signal next activity. Example: Bible for going to church; napkin for going to table for lunch
	Visual schedule with pictures	Visual schedule with pictures
	Keeping materials organized in specific areas	Cleaning up after meals
	Cleaning up after task to signal it is finished	Using tape on the floor to indicate where child is to sit or stand in Sunday school at circle time or story time
	Taping off table areas so child can see boundary	Taping off table areas so child can see boundary
	Clear visual boundaries for where child is to be. Example: using banana box for sitting in during circle time or individual rug, blanket, or place mat	
Answering "wh" questions, "if" questions; retelling stories	Narrating back to teacher what she has read aloud (nonverbal student uses sign language and pictures)	Narrating back stories that parent reads to child using sign language and pictures

Skill	Components of cottage school experience that helped skill to develop	Components of family life experience that helped skill to develop
	Answering questions that teacher asks about a story	Playing with child
	Answering questions during conversations on nature hikes	Taking child everywhere the parent goes and talking to them about everything they are doing
	Teacher uses every opportunity to interact and speak with child: "What color is your coat?" "Where did we go today?" "Who is wearing red?" "What would happen if . . ."	Attending Sunday school with attentive, caring volunteers
Answering questions from peer	Show-and-tell	Allowing sleepovers with typical peers
	Sharing work in front of the class	
Asking peer for assistance	Working in groups	Working with siblings on chores
Offering assistance to peer	Helps with snack, lunch, passing out papers, chores	Helping siblings and parents with household chores

TEACHING TIPS

Behavior	Teaching strategy
Wants to lie down or curl up under table or desk instead of sitting up during story time	Some children may not have good trunk control. If child is listening and not disturbing others, allow alternative postures for attending to tasks.
Disruptive during group activities	Have aid or parent volunteer sit beside child to gently guide them through activity. Analyze whether or not the activity is engaging. Consider allowing child to manipulate quiet toy or do alternate activity at the group table.

Behavior	Teaching strategy
Wiggles too much during class time or meal time	Use a gel seat or large ball for sitting on. Allow child to stand.
Gets "stuck" emotionally; won't let go of an issue they are upset about	Remove child to quiet area with beanbag chair or other soft, comforting chair/area. Do not talk to child because they aren't hearing you. Wait with them to calm down. Use pictures or objects to help communicate what you'd like them to do next. Go for a walk. Jump on trampoline.
Fears field trips	Print pictures of where you're going from the Internet. Create social stories with the photos. In social stories, be specific about where you're going, how you're going, who will be there, and what you will do there.
Doesn't complete homework	Never ban a child from recess for unfinished homework. Children need to move. Communicate with parent via phone, email, or a take-home journal that travels back and forth from home to school. Ask yourself if the homework is absolutely necessary. Parents are exhausted after a long day and adding homework to the many challenges of parenting a child with autism may be unrealistic and too demanding.
Is disruptive during free time	Children with ASD struggle with initiating. Give child two choices of activities for free time. You may need to provide a structured area or a structured work system.
Ignores instruction	Use as few words as possible. The more you talk, the more they won't understand. Use pictures and sign language.
Becomes overwhelmed	Keep lessons short. Teach child to use a "break" symbol to give teacher when they need a break. Provide a break area with pillows, beanbags, headphones, books. Allow child to return when calm. Go for a walk. Jump on trampoline.
Doesn't seem to follow directions	Be specific. "Rinse your glass." "Throw away your napkin." Use as few words as possible. Use pictures as needed.
Has a meltdown between transitions	Use a picture schedule. (See cottage school chart for more ideas on smoothing transitions.)

Behavior	Teaching strategy
Has problems with loud assemblies/activities	Wear headphones. Consider whether or not this activity is absolutely necessary or if child can do an alternative, less stressful activity.
Says "no"	Offer choices such as, "Would you like to work on numbers or would you rather work on letters first?" or "What part of this worksheet should we do first, the top or the bottom?" or "Do you want to color the bird first or cut it out first?"
Is cranky	Is the child hungry or thirsty? Tired? Keep protein snacks available. (Check with parents for allergies.) Allow child to nap for a short time if sleep is needed. (Some children with autism don't sleep well.)
Talks excessively about one topic	Give child a certain amount of poker chips or tokens to "spend" in order to talk about their favorite topic. Let child carry a notebook so that they can write down their thoughts about the topic instead of speaking about it. Set a specific time of day that they are allowed to speak freely about the topic and use a timer to limit the time. Keep a visual "meter" on child's desk to help child know whether or not they are talking too much. Teacher quietly walks to it and moves the hand on the meter.
Is argumentative	If student speaks out of turn to argue with the teacher, ask them to write down their argument/ point of view for the teacher to read later. Paste a list of unacceptable words such as "dumb" or "stupid" on child's desk to remind them not
	to use such words. Remind them it is okay to agree to disagree because people won't always see things the same way. Paste a list of positive words that child can use in their debates. Reinforce positive behavior when it occurs.
Gets angry and upset when schedule is interrupted or unexpected things come up	Rehearse appropriate behavior for when a bus may be late or the weather doesn't allow an activity. Video the appropriate behavior and allow child to watch it. Create social stories about how to react to unexpected situations and disappointments.

Behavior	Teaching strategy
Makes noises that disrupt class	Consider chewing gum if child is able. Does child need a break? Go for a walk or jump on the trampoline. Is there something in the environment child is trying to drown out?
Wanders around the room	Allow child to sit on large ball. Determine what is overstimulating child. Is someone touching them? Talking too loud? Provide child with visual boundaries of where they are to sit or stay such as tape or moveable partitions, or have child sit in a large banana box.

TANTRUM VERSUS MELTDOWN

Tantrum (yes)		Meltdown (no)
✔	Child watching for reaction?	✘
✔	Child considering own safety?	✘
✔	Child in control of own behavior?	✘
✔	Child attempting to communicate needs?	✘
✔	Child calm after issue resolved?	✘

Keep voice calm and even. Use few words. Do not use sarcasm or interact or defend. Do not invoke discipline at this time. Gently, with calm, nonthreatening body language, inform child of what they *can* do, not what they *can't* do. "You can go to the quiet place now." "You can use kind words to speak to me." Remove child to safe place. Child will respond to calm body language and voice more positively than words. (They are not listening much at this time.) Afterward, evaluate the trigger and determine whether or not it can be eliminated. Discuss the situation later with child, with very few words, and use pictures if needed. Role-play with child responding appropriately. Use a video camera and let child watch role-playing of appropriate behavior. Also help child to understand their feelings by using pictures of people showing emotions. Help child understand how the teacher and students felt during their meltdown using pictures as well. Teacher can video her response for child to watch later. Respond to positive behavior with immediate praise. Use an "emotional thermometer" picture that explains different phases of emotions from calm to aroused to agitated to angry. Also use a chart to list "This never bothers me," "This sometimes bothers me," "This makes me feel nervous," "This makes me feel upset," and "This makes me angry." Use emoticon pictures to help child better understand each phase of emotion and what they are feeling.

For more autism behavior tips, explore these websites:

- Pinterest.com
- Teacherspayteachers.com
- Autismspeaks.org
- Helpguide.org
- Centerforautism.com
- Autismteachingstrategies.com
- KarlaAkins.com

Appendix B
Reinforcers and Rewards for School and Home

- Popping a sheet of bubble wrap
- Mini crackers
- Mini chewable candies (for small-step training)
- Buttons with Velcro on the back; child can wear the card they Velcro to a lanyard
- Sticker notebooks (place stickers in a small, flip notebook; when child fills notebook they get a prize)
- Text the teacher on phone
- Play with teacher's/parent's phone (or classroom phone or tablet)
- Facetime with the teacher (on phone or tablet)
- Phone call with the teacher
- Get to be the teacher for thirty minutes (or other preferred amount of time)
- No-homework pass
- Extra computer time
- Choose music for free time
- Choose video for afternoon/class party
- Wear hat in class
- Wear pajamas to school
- Be first in line
- Make sculptures with duct tape
- New magazine of choice
- New poster
- Play chess one-on-one with teacher or parent
- Play favorite app on iPad or tablet
- Choose dessert or menu for holiday party
- Pick what color teacher or parent will wear next day
- Warm fuzzies
- Marbles in a jar
- New pen or pencil
- Reward coupons

- Tokens to save up for prizes
- Toy money to exchange for things in the prize box
- Free tardy pass
- Pizza party
- Visit to the park
- Eat outdoors
- Punch cards
- Soda/favorite drink in class
- Extra time to play with Legos or other favorite activity
- Later bedtime
- Parent does child's chore(s)
- Bring stuffed animal to school
- Extra show-and-tell
- No shoes day
- A jar filled with privileges written on small tokens; student draws one for a reward
- Sit at the teacher's desk
- Special snack
- Draw on the chalkboard/whiteboard/smartboard
- Extra marbles for class marble jar
- Teacher's assistant for the day
- Lunch/snack/dinner with the teacher
- Operate the remote control for the DVD player
- Take pictures of the class on field-trip day
- Play with stamps
- Special reward handshake with teacher or parent
- Doughnuts for breakfast
- Snowball fight with cotton balls
- Pillow fight
- Sit by friend in class
- Free points toward credit on a wrong answer on a test
- Paint class window
- Play with water outdoors
- Read a book to the class or family
- Be the calendar teacher for the day
- Be the "technician" for the day (turn lights on and off, start visual equipment, etc.)
- Help in the kitchen
- Sit in favorite spot or chair
- Sit in teacher's desk
- Choose recess to be indoors or outdoors
- Use special supplies reserved only for reward use
- Queen or king for the day— wear a crown or badge
- Take a nap

Appendix C
Fidget Toys

- Mini trampoline
- Fill socks with rice and tie them off; lay them on child's lap to help them sit still
- Microwaveable heat packs for lap or shoulders
- Bungee cords around chair legs (child can pull with feet/legs)
- Hacky Sacks (to keep hands busy)
- Fingerless gloves with light weights attached (can use heavy washers)
- Snow globe
- Beanie Babies
- Slinky
- Beanbags
- Rubber ducky
- Legos
- Linking toys
- Bendable action figures
- Balloons filled with rice or sand or play dough
- Hand puppets
- Sponges
- Toy cars or trucks (hand-sized)
- Play dough
- Pencil grips
- Chew toys
- Bubble wrap
- Smooth stones
- Shells
- Plush toys
- Paper clips
- Bumpy tubing

Anything that is quiet and keeps hands or feet busy during class time can be used. The possibilities are as endless as your imagination. For younger children, be careful of choking hazards. Also, if a child puts items in their mouth, be sure they are lead free.

Appendix D
Functional Skills Checklist

Typical children may learn reading, writing, and mathematics in order to progress to higher levels of learning. Children with cognitive or neurological disabilities need these skills to be independent in everyday living. For example, to follow a recipe one must know how to read. To purchase ingredients for a recipe, one must be able to read prices, select the correct amount of change, and read a receipt. A student must know how to sign their name to have a bank account. Here are a few goals you may want to include in your child's curriculum or IEP, depending on their age, strengths, and abilities. This list is not at all exhaustive. Your local school district may have a more extensive list.

Writing
- Recognizes/prints/writes lowercase and uppercase letters
- Recognizes/prints/writes name
- Recognizes/prints/writes words (with or without copying)
- Recognizes/prints/writes sentences (with or without copying)
- Recognizes/prints/writes names of family members and friends
- Recognizes/prints/writes address and phone number
- Recognizes/prints/writes simple letter
- Prints/writes an address on an envelope
- Prints/writes résumé

• Fills in forms, such as job applications, banking slips, or clinic admission forms

Reading

• First, middle, and last name
• Names of friends and family members
• Address and telephone number
• Menus
• Community signs/store signs/environmental phrases
• Road signs (and knows their meanings)
• Food labels
• Weather reports
• Appliances (off/on, temperature)

Mathematics

• Recognizes numbers
• Can count (as high as ability allows)
• Simple addition and subtraction
• Use of a calculator
• Banking
• Money values
• Telling time (both digital and analog)
• Temperature
• Classifying/sorting
• Volume and capacity (more/less)
• Miles per hour
• Padlock functions
• Measurement (long/short)

Communication

Receptive Language: Attentive Listening

• Parents
• Teachers

- Therapists
- Siblings
- Peers
- Television
- Radio
- Stories, jokes, riddles
- Sounds in environment
- Warning sounds such as sirens or whistles
- Music

Expressive Language
   Oral Communication
- Uses appropriate vocabulary
- Articulates clearly
- Takes turns in conversations
- Stays on topic
- Expresses ideas clearly
- Asks questions
- Gives information
- Uses correct sentence structure

Augmentative Communication (usually for nonverbal students or students with articulation issues)
- Sign language
- Picture communication systems
- Computer/iPad/tablet technology

Interpersonal Skills

Interpersonal skills are the hardest for people with autism to grasp. Here are a few goals that you may want to include in your child's curriculum or IEP, depending on their strengths, age, and abilities. This list is not meant to be exhaustive. Your local school district may have a more extensive list.

- Responds to introductions and answers simple questions
- Can identify one friend
- Looks others in the eye and shakes hands if other person offers
- Makes small talk (face-to-face)
- Makes introductions
- Is aware of boundary issues
- Is not harmful to others
- Asks for help
- Explains feelings
- Can identify relationships that may be hurtful or dangerous
- Accepts invitations from others to be involved in social activities
- Makes arrangements with peers for social activities
- Knows where to get help if unable to resolve interpersonal conflicts
- Has some ability to resolve conflicts with others
- Refrains from physical violence as a means of solving interpersonal conflict
- Has practiced and is able to say no to peers who are trying to persuade him/her to do something wrong
- Avoids hurtful or dangerous relationships
- Labels and expresses anger or other strong feelings appropriately; "talks out" problems

Independent Living Skills

Every parent hopes their child will be independent one day. As your child nears their teens, depending on their level of functioning, you may want to focus a bit more on these skills. Here are a few independent living skills goals you may want to include in your child's curriculum or IEP, depending on their strengths, age, and abilities. This list is not at all exhaustive. Your local school district may have a more extensive list.

Self-Care
- Showers/bathes thoroughly
- Brushes teeth

- Can dress self in a reasonably acceptable fashion (including underwear, socks, and tied shoes)
- Knows how to use soap, shampoo, deodorant, shaving cream, and other common personal products
- Toilets self

Health and Safety
- Knows to lock doors
- Carries and safely produces an ID card
- Knows personal information (phone number, address, etc.)
- Recognizes law enforcers, their uniforms, badges, and vehicles
- Knows how to respond to law enforcement, customs and immigration, and first responders, such as fire rescue, paramedics, hospital emergency room professionals, or other security professionals
- Knows how to respond to symptoms of illness, accidents, or emergencies
- Knows how to access emergency shelter
- Uses phone for emergencies
- Uses basic first aid
- Accesses and uses medical professionals
- Uses public toilets
- Discloses their ASD (e.g., carrying and producing an autism information card)
- Follows medication directions and orders refills
- Knows not to take someone else's medication
- Knows the dangers of drugs, alcohol, and tobacco
- Knows parts of the body and sexual functioning
- Knows how pregnancy occurs

Nutrition
- Washes hands before eating and preparing food
- Orders at a fast-food restaurant
- Orders a meal from the menu in a restaurant

- Knows name and use of cooking utensils
- Fixes breakfast/lunch/dinner for one
- Makes out a grocery shopping list
- Uses cooking utensils effectively and safely
- Uses kitchen appliances effectively and safely
- Knows and uses acceptable table manners
- Stores perishable items in refrigerator
- Recognizes spoiled food
- Follows instructions for preparing canned or frozen foods
- Plans weekly menu of nutritious meals
- Shops for a week's menu and stays within a food budget
- Sets table properly

Money Management
- Knows values of coins and currency
- Makes a transaction at a local store and is able to count change
- Understands the difference between luxuries and necessities
- Understands the difference between sale price and regular price
- Uses a calculator to add, subtract, divide, and multiply
- Makes out monthly budget with assistance
- Clips and uses coupons

Household Management
- Washes dishes adequately, using soap and hot water
- Changes a light bulb
- Makes bed
- Knows how to dispose of garbage
- Uses vacuum cleaner properly and empties dirt receptacle
- Changes bed linen
- Knows how to prevent sinks and toilets from clogging and how to unclog them
- Sweeps floor and stairs, washes wood and linoleum floors, washes windows, and dusts and polishes furniture

- Cleans toilet, bathtub, and sink
- Uses appropriate cleaning products
- Knows how to get rid of and avoid roaches, ants, mice, and other pests

Transportation
- Understands and uses seat belts
- Is familiar with any form of public transportation available
- Can give directions
- Arranges routine transportation to work or school
- Reads a map

Legal Issues
- Knows phone number of someone to call if arrested or victimized
- Understands what actions are against the law and what the consequences are
- Knows personal rights if arrested
- Knows what the function of a lawyer is
- Knows legal age for buying alcohol and tobacco products
- Understands the meaning of "legal age" in legal terms (what you can do, what you cannot do)
- Knows how and where to register to vote
- Is registered to vote
- Knows where to go to vote
- Knows the legal penalty for all of the following: buying, possessing, selling, and doing drugs; buying and drinking beer and alcohol under age; trespassing, shoplifting, burglary, possession of stolen property, traffic violations, and assault

Appendix E
Further Resources

Books About Autism

1001 Great Ideas for Teaching and Raising Children with Autism or Asperger's by Ellen Notbohm and Veronica Zysk

Autism's Hidden Blessings: Discovering God's Promises for Autistic Children and Their Families by Kelly Langston

Autism and Your Church: Nurturing the Spiritual Growth of People with Autism Spectrum Disorder by Barbara J. Newman

The Autism Trail Guide: Postcards from the Road Less Traveled by Ellen Notbohm

The Autistic Brain: Helping Different Kinds of Minds Succeed by Temple Grandin

The Child with Special Needs: Encouraging Intellectual and Emotional Growth by Stanley I. Greenspan and Robin Simons

Engaging Autism: Using the Floortime Approach to Help Children Relate, Communicate, and Think by Stanley I. Greenspan and Serena Wieder

How to Teach Life Skills to Kids with Autism and Asperger's by Jennifer McIlwee Myers

Leading a Special Needs Ministry by Amy Fenton Lee

The New Social Story Book by Carol Gray

The Out-of-Sync Child: Recognizing and Coping with Sensory Processing Disorder by Carol Kranowitz

The Out-of-Sync Child Has Fun: Activities for Kids with Sensory Processing Disorder by Carol Kranowitz

The Special Needs Ministry Handbook: A Church's Guide to Reaching Children with Disabilities and Their Families by Amy Rapada

Ten Things Every Child with Autism Wishes You Knew by Ellen Notbohm

Thinking in Pictures: My Life with Autism by Temple Grandin

Understanding Autism for Dummies by Stephen Shore and Linda G. Rastelli

The Way I See It: A Personal Look at Autism and Asperger's by Temple Grandin

A Few of Karla's Favorite Books on Homeschooling

A Charlotte Mason Companion: Personal Reflections on the Gentle Art of Learning by Karen Andreola

Emily Post's Etiquette by Emily Post

Handbook of Nature Study by Anna Botsford Comstock

Homeschooling for Dummies by Jennifer Kaufield

Keeping a Nature Journal: Discover a Whole New Way of Seeing the World Around You by Clare Walker Leslie and Charles E. Roth

Pocketful of Pinecones: Nature Study with the Gentle Art of Learning by Karen Andreola

Teaching the Trivium: Christian Homeschooling in a Classical Style by Harvey Bluedorn and Laurie Bluedorn

The Well-Educated Mind: A Guide to the Classical Education You Never Had by Susan Wise Bauer

The Well-Trained Mind: A Guide to Classical Christian Education at Home by Susan Wise Bauer and Jessie Wise

Karla's Favorite Read-Aloud Books

This is not an exhaustive list, but these are some of the favorites of my children and students at our cottage school.

Adam of the Road by Elizabeth Gray Vining

Anne of Green Gables (eight-book series) by L. M. Montgomery

Are You My Mother? by P. D. Eastman

Beowulf: A Verse Translation by Frederick Rebsamen

The Boxcar Children series by Gertrude Chandler Warner

The Burgess Animal Book for Children by Thornton W. Burgess

The Burgess Bird Book for Children by Thornton W. Burgess

The Burgess Seashore Book for Children by Thornton W. Burgess (All books by Thornton Burgess come highly recommended!)

Castle Diary: The Journal of Tobias Burgess by Richard Platt

The Cat of Bubastes: A Tale of Ancient Egypt by G. A. Henty

Charlotte's Web by E. B. White

A Child's Garden of Verses by Robert Louis Stevenson

Corduroy by Don Freeman

The Door in the Wall by Marguerite De Angeli

Dude, That's Rude! (Get Some Manners) by Pamela Espeland and Elizabeth Verdick

Freckles by Gene Stratton-Porter

A Girl of the Limberlost by Gene Stratton-Porter

The Golden Goblet by Eloise Jarvis McGraw

Goodbye, Mr. Chips by James Hilton

Harry the Dirty Dog by Gene Zion

The Hedge of Thorns (Lamplighter Rare Collector's Series edition) edited by Mark Hamby

If You Give a Mouse a Cookie by Laura Joffe Numeroff

Jesse Bear, What Will You Wear? by Nancy White Carlstrom

Little House on the Prairie series by Laura Ingalls Wilder

Little Men by Louisa May Alcott

The Little Mouse, the Red Ripe Strawberry, and the Big Hungry Bear by Don Wood and Audrey Wood

Little Pilgrim's Progress from John Bunyan's Classic by Helen L. Taylor

Little Women by Louisa May Alcott

The Making of a Knight by Patrick O'Brien

Marguerite Makes a Book by Bruce Robertson

The Miraculous Journey of Edward Tulane by Kate DiCamillo

Misty of Chincoteague by Marguerite Henry

Mr. Popper's Penguins by Richard Atwater
Nick of Time by Ted Bell
Once on This Island by Gloria Whelan
Robinson Crusoe by Daniel Defoe
Rosa of Linden Castle by Christoph von Schmid
Seaman's Journal by Gail Langer Karwoski
Song of Roland by Dorothy Sayers
Squanto and the Miracle of Thanksgiving by Eric Metaxas
Stuart Little by E. B. White
The Tale of Despereaux by Kate DiCamillo
Winnie-the-Pooh by A. A. Milne
The Wolf's Chicken Stew by Keiko Kasza
The Year of Miss Agnes by Kirkpatrick Hill

Read-Aloud Narrative History Books by Karla Akins
Jacques Cartier
O Canada! Her Story
Sacagawea
What Really Happened in Ancient Times
What Really Happened in Colonial Times
What Really Happened in the Middle Ages

Karla's Favorite Homeschool/School Curriculums
A Beka Book (for beginning readers): *abeka.com/HomeSchool/SubjectInfo
/Reading.aspx*
Ambleside Online (free Charlotte Mason guidelines): *amblesideonline.org*
Dover Publications (for coloring books and art books): *store.doverpubli
cations.com*
Grapevine Studies: *grapevinestudies.com*
Handwriting Without Tears: *hwtears.com/hwt*
Heart of Wisdom: *heartofwisdom.com/blog*
Homeschool in the Woods: *homeschoolinthewoods.com*
Hooked on Phonics: *hookedonphonics.com*

Knowledge Quest: *knowledgequestmaps.com*
KONOS: *konos.com/www*
Math-U-See: *mathusee.com*
Mystery of History: *themysteryofhistory.com*
Signing Exact English: *seecenter.org*
Teachers Pay Teachers: *teacherspayteachers.com*
Tucker Signing Strategies for Reading—New Edition: *ahaprocess.com/store
   /tucker-signing-strategies-for-reading-new-edition-manual-dvd/*

Special-Needs Ministry Websites

Friendship Ministries: *friendship.org*
Joni and Friends: *joniandfriends.org*
Joni and Friends Family Retreats (highly recommended!): *joniandfriends
   .org/family-retreats*
PURE Ministries: *pure-ministries.com*
Through the Roof Ministries: *throughtheroof.org*

Helpful Homeschool Websites

Homeschool Legal Defense Association: *hslda.org/strugglinglearner*
NATHHAN: National Challenged Homeschoolers Associated Network:
   nathhan.com
Simply Charlotte Mason: *simplycharlottemason.com/store*
The Well-Trained Mind: *welltrainedmind.com*

Helpful Websites

Autism Classroom News (lots of great ideas): *autismclassroomresources.com
   /autism-classroom-news/*
Autism Love to Know (free lesson plans): *autism.lovetoknow.com/Free
   _Lesson_Plans_for_Autistic_Kids*
Carol Gray Social Stories: *carolgraysocialstories.com*
Do 2 Learn: *do2learn.com*
Fetal Alcohol Spectrum Disorders: *come-Over.to/FASCRC*
Floortime Therapy: *stanleygreenspan.com/about-floortime*

Geneva Center for Autism: *autism.net*
Handy Handouts: *handyhandouts.com*
Heart of Wisdom's Pinterest Workboxes Page: *pinterest.com/heartofwisdom /homeschool-workboxes*
Infant Massage: *infantmassageusa.org*
Learning Abled Kids: *learningabledkids.com*
Parenting Asperger's Community: *parentingaspergerscommunity.com*
Picture Exchange Communication System: *pecsusa.com*
Practical Autism Resources (printables): *practicalautismresources.com/printables*
Sensory Processing Disorder: *sensory-processing-disorder.com*
Sensory Smarts: *sensorysmarts.com*
SEN Teacher: *senteacher.org*
SPD Foundation: *spdnow.org*
Sue Patrick's Workbox System: *workboxsystem.com*
Temple Grandin: *templegrandin.com*
Therapy Street for Kids: *therapystreetforkids.com*
Tony Attwood: *tonyattwood.com.au/*
Treatment and Education of Autistic and Communication Related Handicapped Children: *teacch.com*
Vaccination Information: *vactruth.com*
Watch Me Learn: *watchmelearn.com*
WrightsLaw (A plethora of information regarding special education and laws): *wrightslaw.com*

Helpful Blogs

Adventures in Autism: *adventuresinautism.blogspot.com*
Ashi's Gift: *ashisgift.blogspot.com/*
Autism and More: *sharonscreativecorner.com/autismblog/*
Autism Light: *autism-light.blogspot.com*
Autism Speaks: *autismspeaks.org/blog*
Embrace Your Chaos: *facebook.com/embraceyourchaos/*
Flappiness Is: *flappinessis.com*
Horse OT: *horseot.blogspot.com*

Into the Woods: *jennyalice.com*
Karla Akins: *karlaakins.com*
Life with Autism: *michellemguppy.blogspot.com*
Mama OT: *mamaot.com/*
Milestone Mom: *adhdmomma.com/tag/milestone-mom*
Miss Mancy's Blog: *missmancy.com*
OT Café: *abbypediatricot.blogspot.com*
Pedro Javier: *pedrojavier.org*
The Recycling Occupational Therapist: *recyclingot.blogspot.com*
Talk It Up: *talkituptherapy.blogspot.com*
We Go with Him: *autism.typepad.com/autism/*
Your Therapy Source: *yourtherapysource.com/blog1*

Autism Applications for iOS and Android
Articulation Station: *littlebeespeech.com*
Autism Xpress: *autismxpress.com*
Fizz Brain: *fizzbrain.com*
PECS: *pecsusa.com/apps.php*
Proloquo2go: *assistiveware.com/product/proloquo2go*

Apps for iPad
ABA Flashcards and Games
Autism and PDD Reasoning and Problem Solving
Autism iHelp
Autism Tracker
iCreate
iGet
iRewardChart
Model Me Kids

Apps for Kindle Fire/Android
AAC Speech Communicator
Autism iHelp

Autism Speech DiegoSays
Behavior Status
Days Sequence
IEP Goals
JABTalk
Show Me
Speech Companion Speech Therapy
TFA—Tools for Autism

Autism Organizations

Action for Autism (India): *autism-india.org*

Association for Science in Autism Treatment (ASAT): *asatonline.org*

Autism Consortium: *autismconsortium.org*

Autism National Committee: *autcom.org*

Autism Research Institute (ARI): *autism.com*

Autism Society of America (ASA): *autism-society.org*

Autism Speaks: *autismspeaks.org*

Autistica: *autistica.org.uk*

Daniel Jordan Fiddle Foundation for Adult Autism: *djfiddlefoundation.org*

Doug Flutie Jr. Foundation for Autism: *flutiefoundation.org*

Families for Early Autism Treatment (FEAT): *feat.org*

First Signs: *firstsigns.org*

Generation Rescue: *generationrescue.org*

HollyRod Foundation for Help and Hope: *hollyrod.org*

National Association of Residential Providers for Adults with Autism: *narpaa.org*

National Autism Association (NAA): *nationalautismassociation.org*

Organization for Autism Research (OAR): *researchautism.org*

Rethink Autism: *rethinkfirst.com*

Southwest Autism Research & Resource Center (SARRC): *autismcenter.org*

Talk About Curing Autism (TACA): *tacanow.org*

Train4Autism: *train4autism.org*

Notes

Chapter 2: Sea of Grief
1. Leann E. Smith et al., "Daily Experiences Among Mothers of Adolescents and Adults with Autism Spectrum Disorder," *Journal of Autism and Developmental Disorders* 40, no. 2 (2010): 167–78, doi: 10.1007/s10803-009-0844-y.

Chapter 3: God Is Up to Something Good
1. Used by permission, "Up to Something Good," written by Nancy Honeytree Miller, published by OakTable Publishing, Inc. © 1993.

Chapter 4: What Is Autism?
1. Centers for Disease Control and Prevention, "Facts about ASD," last modified March 28, 2016, http://www.cdc.gov/ncbddd/autism/facts.html.
2. American Psychiatric Association, *Diagnostic and Statistical Manual of Mental Disorders*, 5th ed. (Arlington: American Psychiatric Publishing, 2013), 50–59.
3. Rich Stoner et al., "Patches of Disorganization in the Neocortex of Children with Autism," *The New England Journal of Medicine* 370 (2014): 1209–19, doi: 10.1056/NEJMoa1307491.
4. Deborah L. Christensen et al., "Prevalence and Characteristics of Autism Spectrum Disorder Among Children Aged 8 Years—Autism and Developmental Disabilities Monitoring Network, 11 Sites,

United States, 2012," *Morbidity and Mortality Weekly Report* 65, no. 3 (2016): 1–23, doi: http://dx.doi.org/10.15585/mmwr.ss6503a1.

5. Andrew T. Cavagnaro, "Autistic Spectrum Disorders: Changes in the California Caseload: An Update: June 1987–June 2007," California Health and Human Services Agency, http://www.dds.ca.gov /Autism/docs/AutismReport_2007.pdf.

6. Autism Society, "Facts and Statistics," last modified August 26, 2015, https://www.autism-society.org/what-is/facts-and-statistics/.

Chapter 8: Make the Screaming Stop

1. Sensory-Processing-Disorder.com, "Sensory Processing Disorder: Signs and Symptoms of SPD in Infants and Toddlers," accessed May 1, 2017, http://www.sensory-processing-disorder.com/sensory -processing-disorder-checklist.

Chapter 11: Diets, Vaccines, and Medications

1. Fangjun Zhou et al., "Economic Evaluation of the Routine Childhood Immunization Program in the United States, 2009," *Pediatrics* 133, no. 4 (February 2014): 577–85, doi: 10.1542/peds.2013-0698.

2. American Academy of Pediatrics, "Why Immunize Your Child," last modified November 21, 2015, https://www.healthychildren.org /English/safety-prevention/immunizations/Pages/Why-Immunize -Your-Child.aspx.

3. Mead v. Secretary of Health and Human Services, 03-215V (USCFC Spec Mstr 2010), p. 164, http://www.uscfc.uscourts.gov /sites/default/files/opinions/Campbell-Smith%20Mead%20 Autism%20Decision.pdf.

4. Every Child By Two, "Economic Benefits," accessed May 1, 2017, http://www.ecbt.org/index.php/facts_and_issues/article/economic _benefits.

5. Sharyl Attkisson, "How Independent Are Vaccine Defenders?," CBS, July 25, 2008, http://www.cbsnews.com/news/how-independent -are-vaccine-defenders/.

6. The College of Physicians of Philadelphia, "Human Cell Strains in Vaccine Development," last modified April 19, 2017, http://www .historyofvaccines.org/content/articles/human-cell-strains-vaccine -development.

Chapter 13: Little Cottage School on the Prairie
1. Charlotte Mason, quoted in Margaret A. Coombs, *Charlotte Mason: Hidden Heritage and Education Influence* (Cambridge: Lutterworth Press, 2015), 187.

Karla Akins is the mother of five, two of which are twin sons with autism. She has a bachelor's in special education from Western Governors University and a doctorate in Christian education from Kingsway Theological Seminary. She is the author of five books, including her first novel, *The Pastor's Wife Wears Biker Boots*, which features a homeschool mom and a child with autism. Karla is a teacher and popular speaker at conferences and retreats. She enjoys riding her motorcycle, sipping chai lattes, and snuggling with her three dogs and two cats. Karla loves hearing from her readers. You can contact her at KarlaAkins.com.